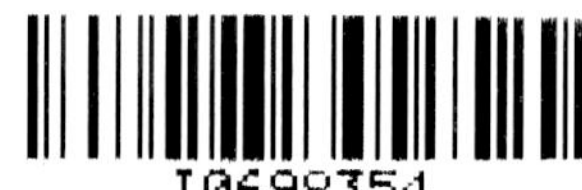


I am grateful to God for everything! And I believe that the meaning of life is to make sense of other lives. C.A., you are the meaning of my life.
Lov U

Lucas Dias
2024

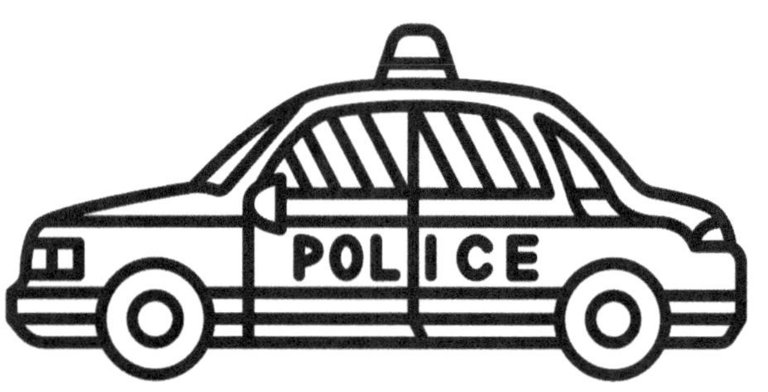
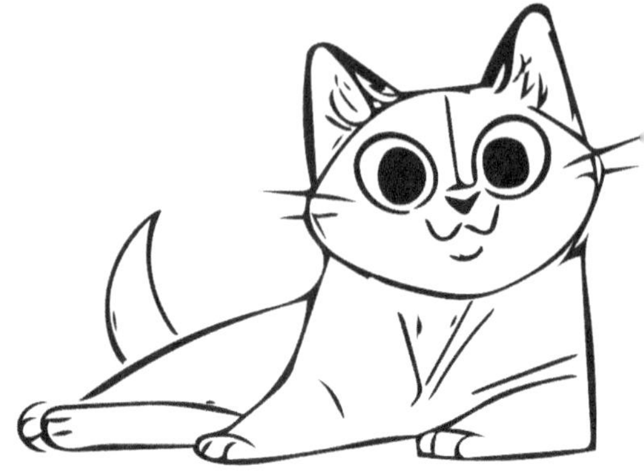

# This Book Belongs to:

_______________________

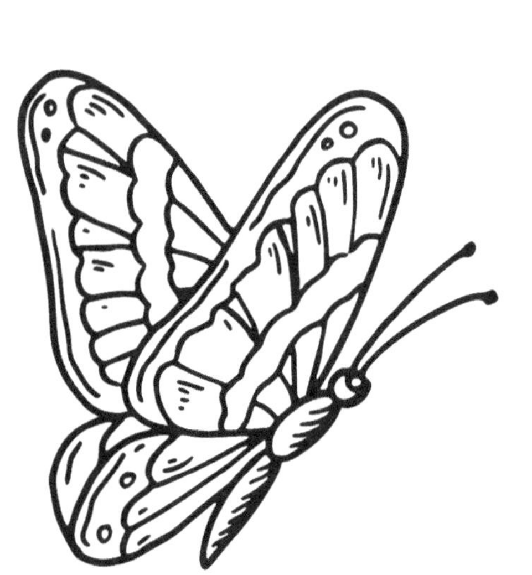
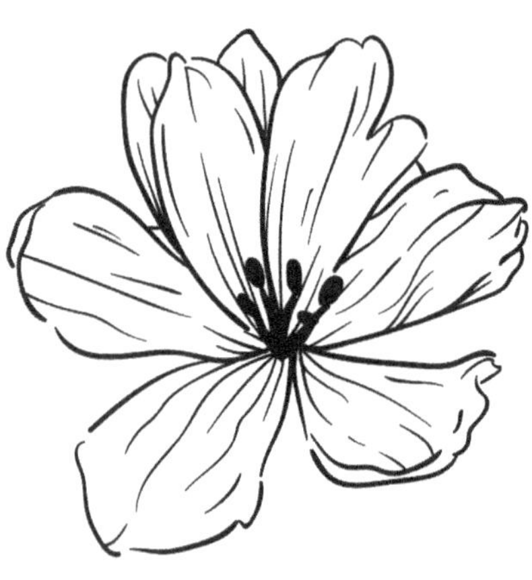
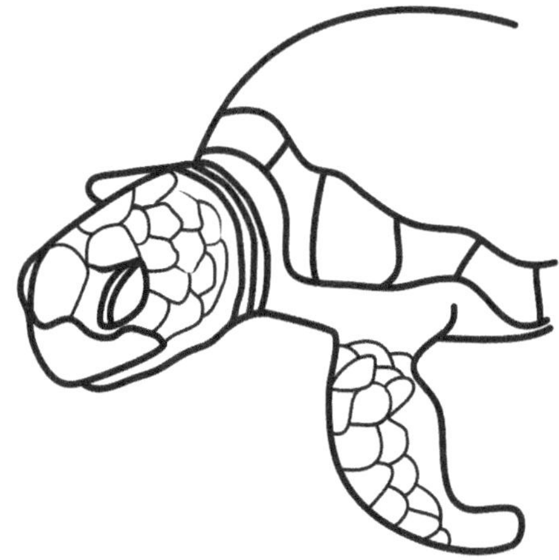

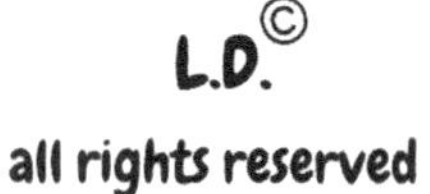

# Test Color Page

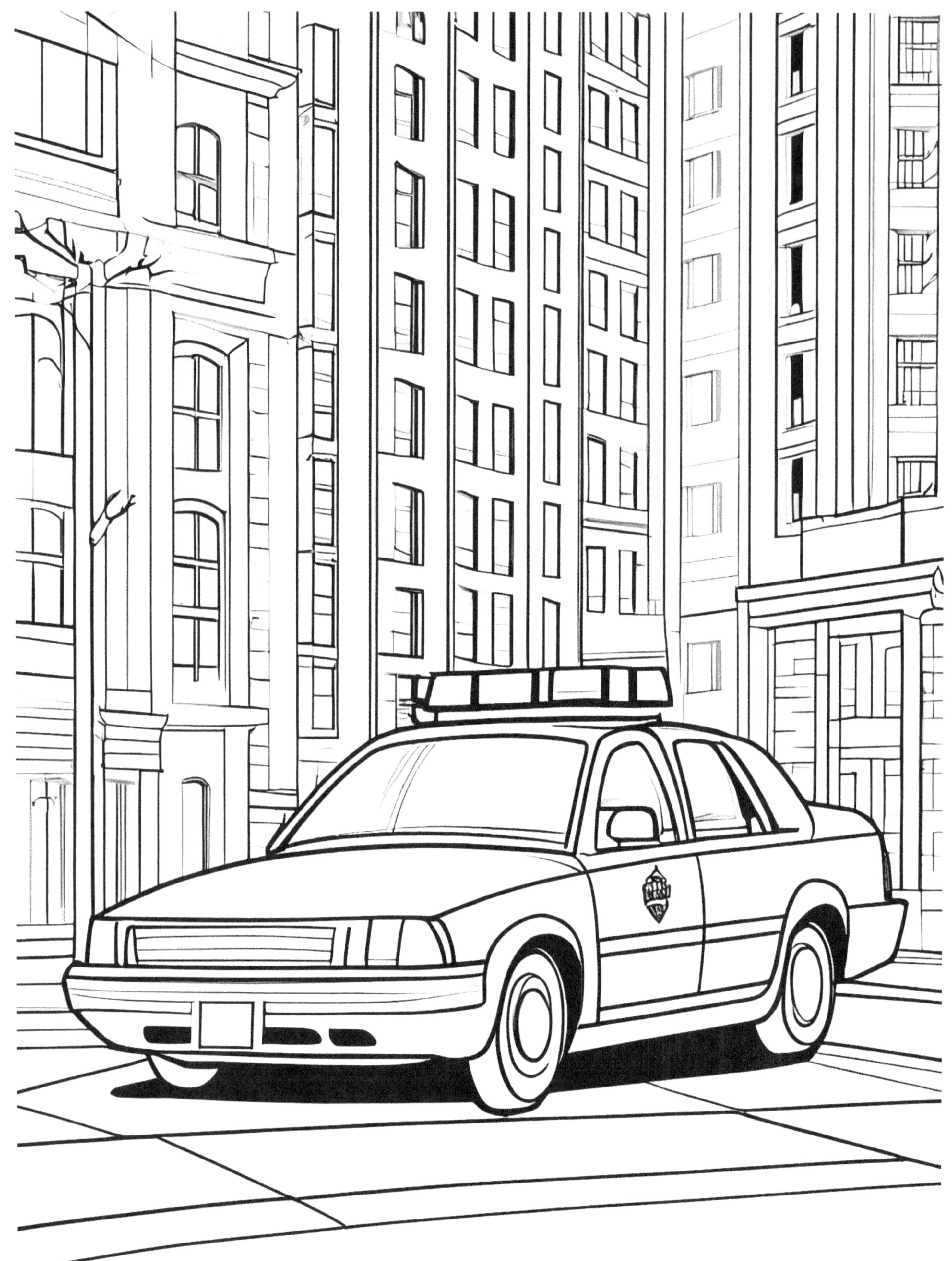

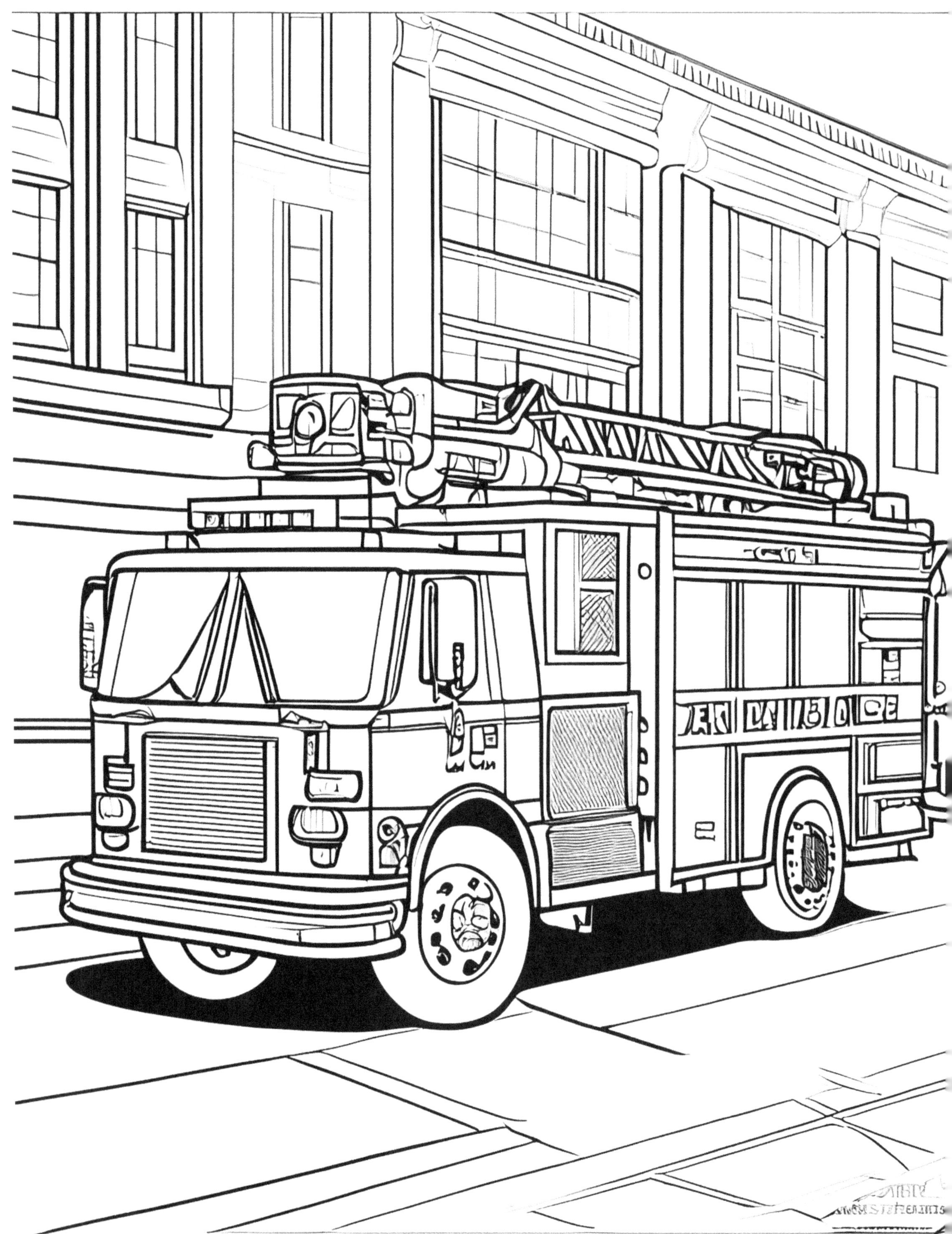

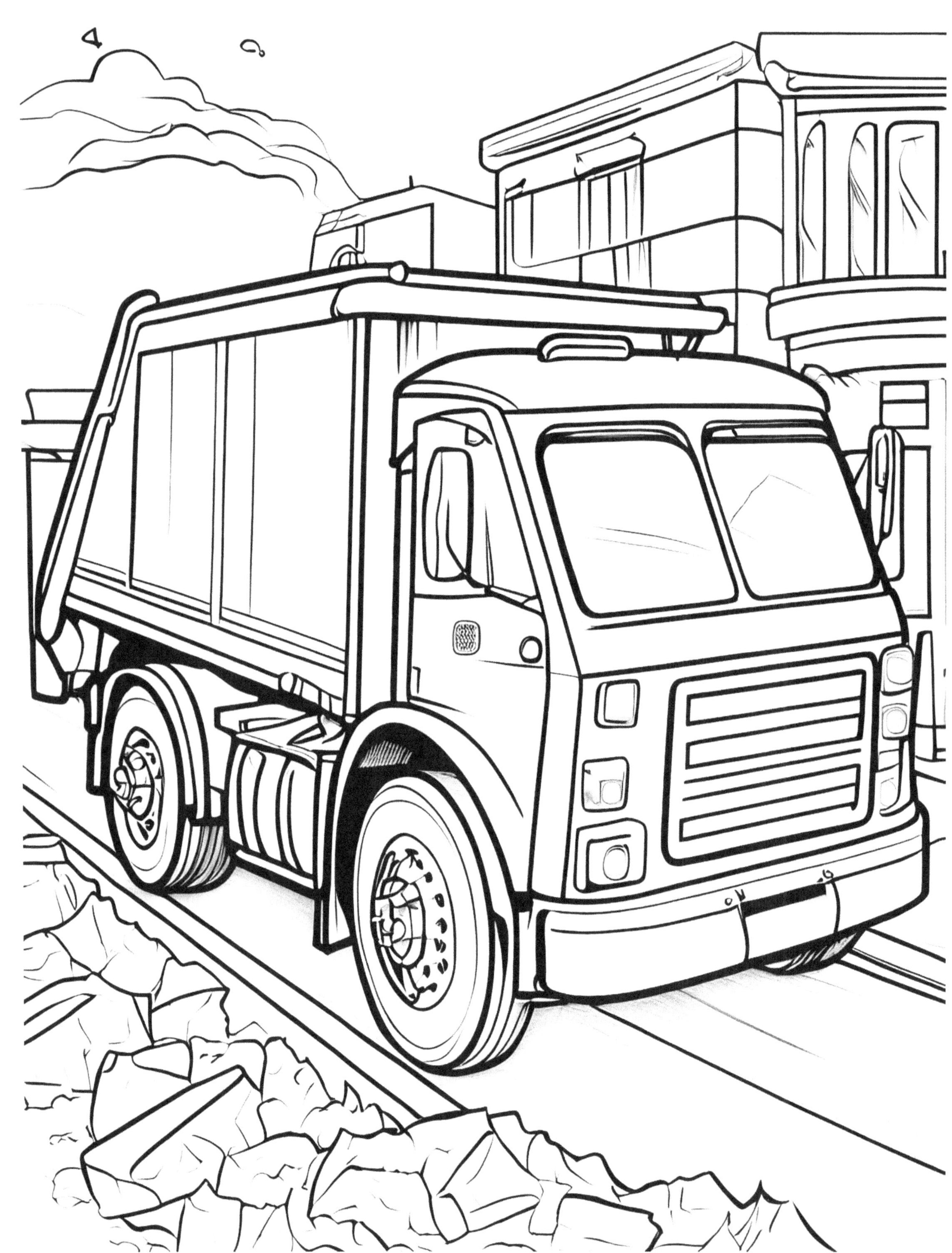

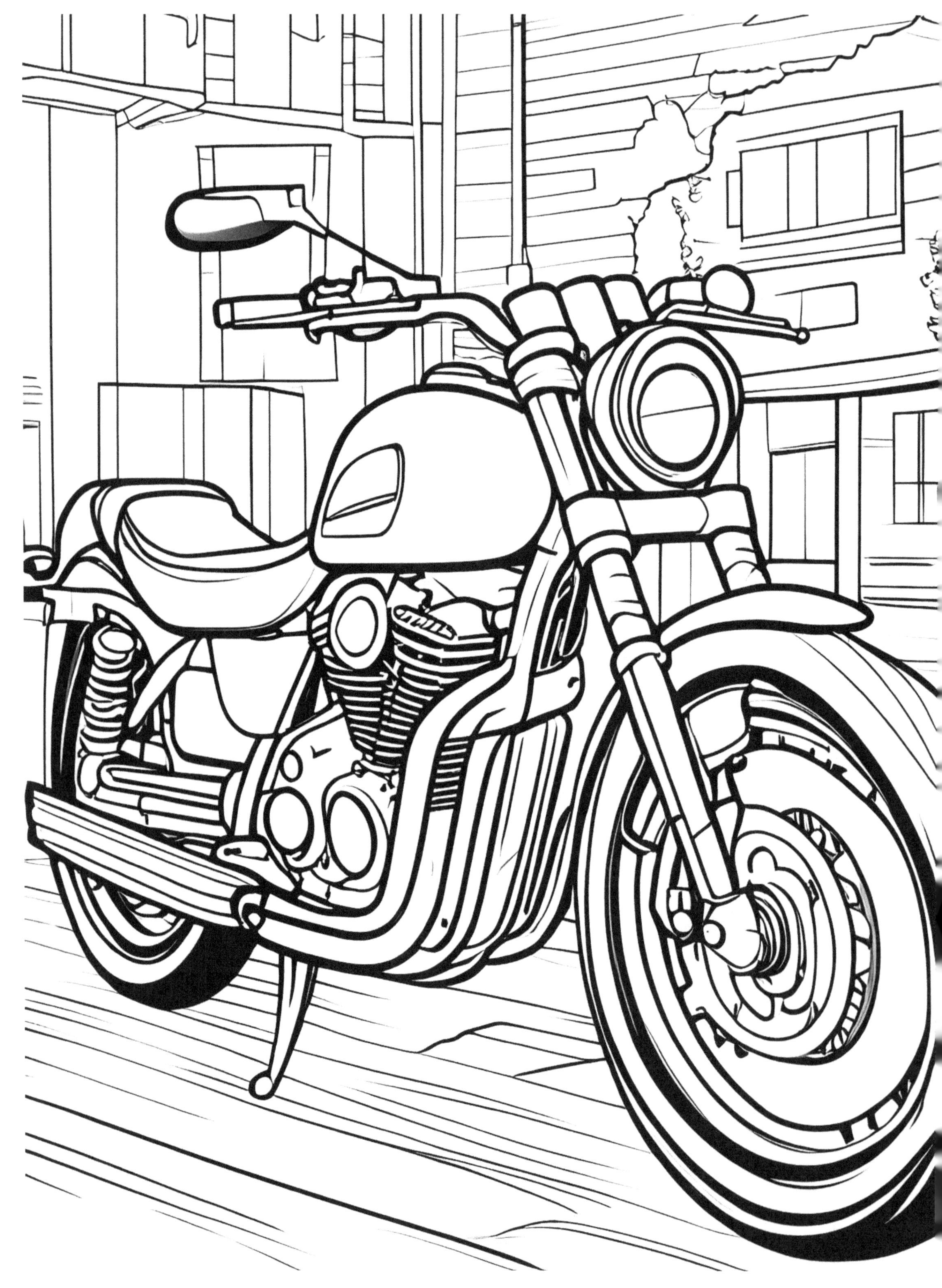

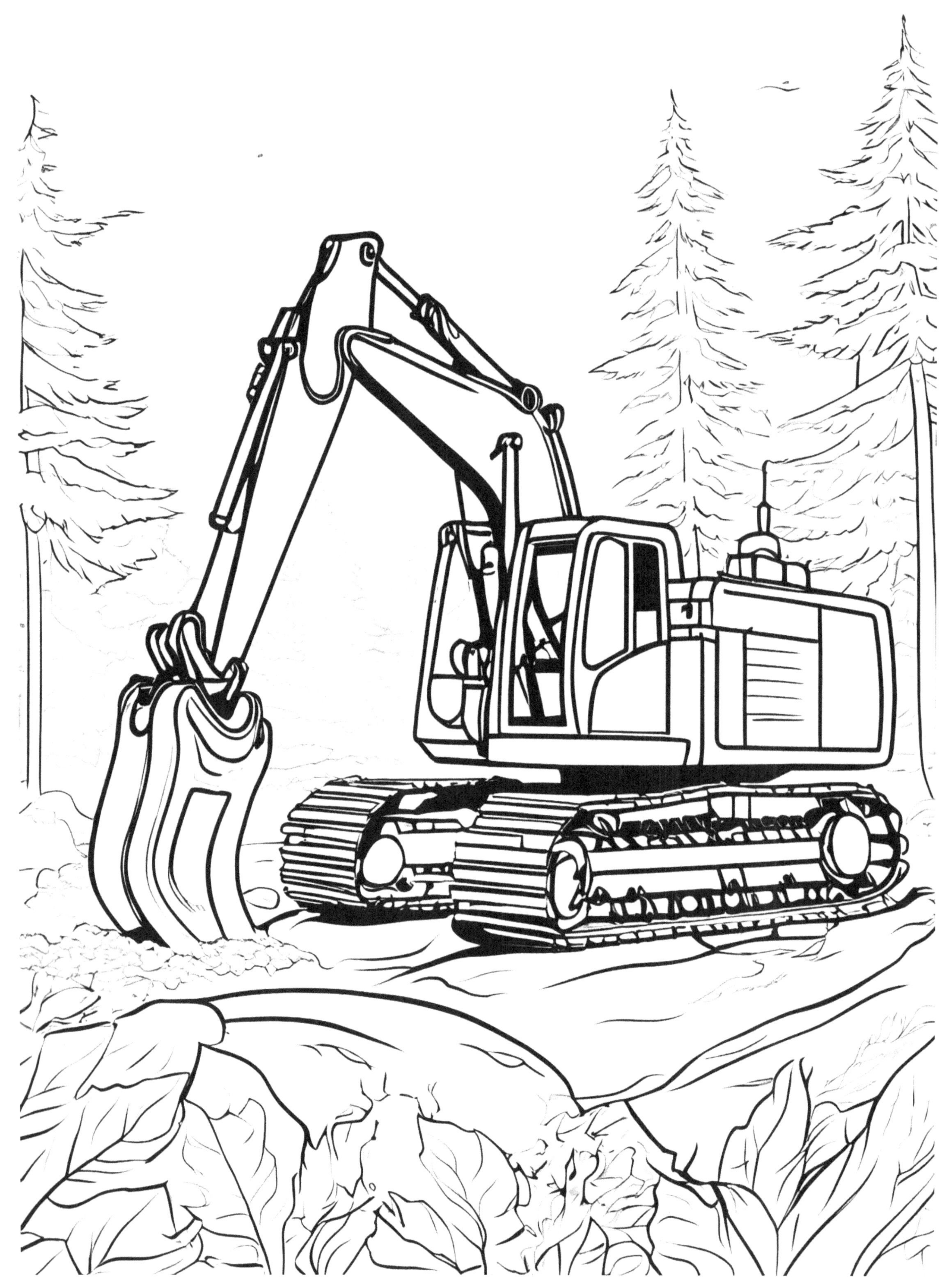

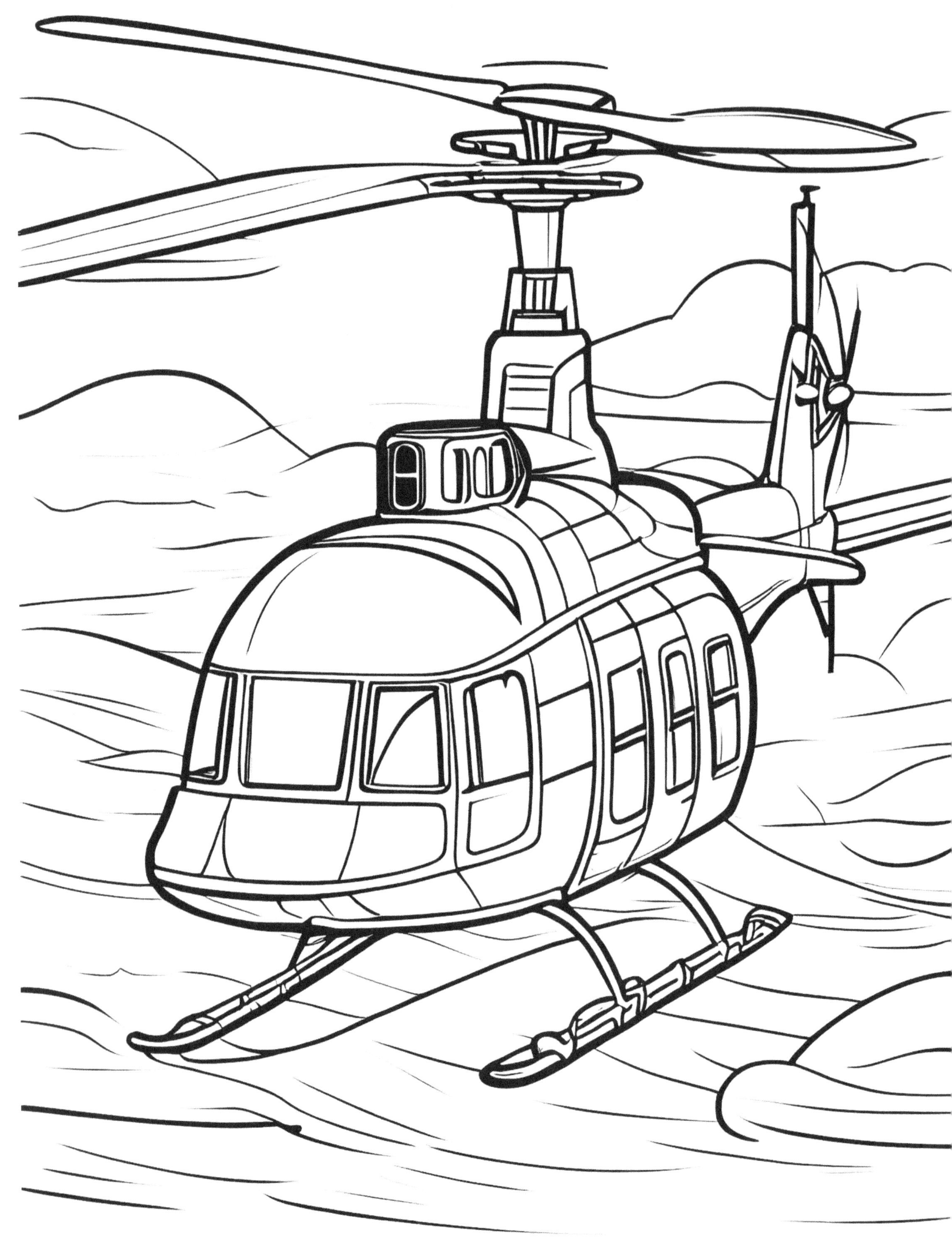

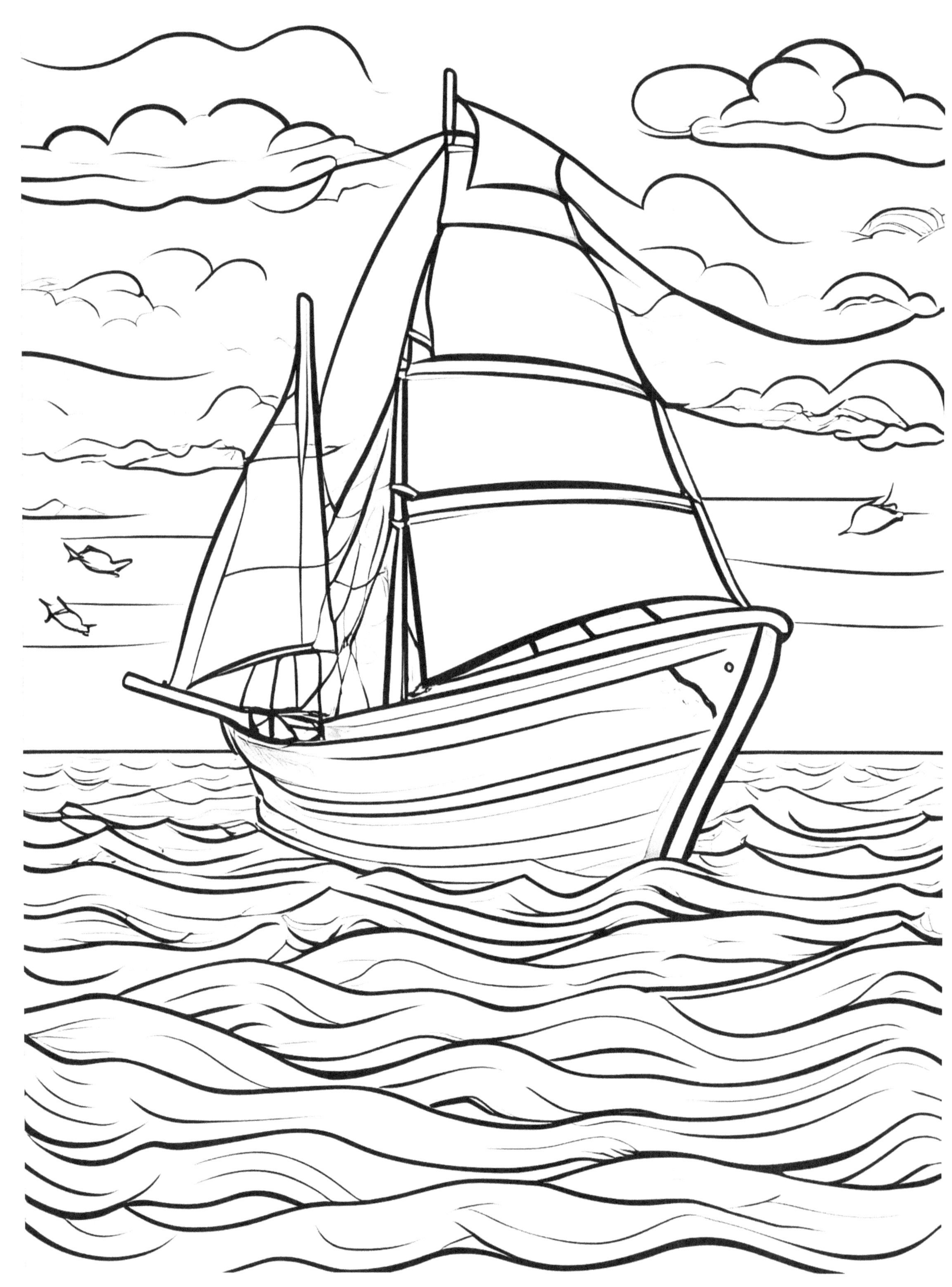

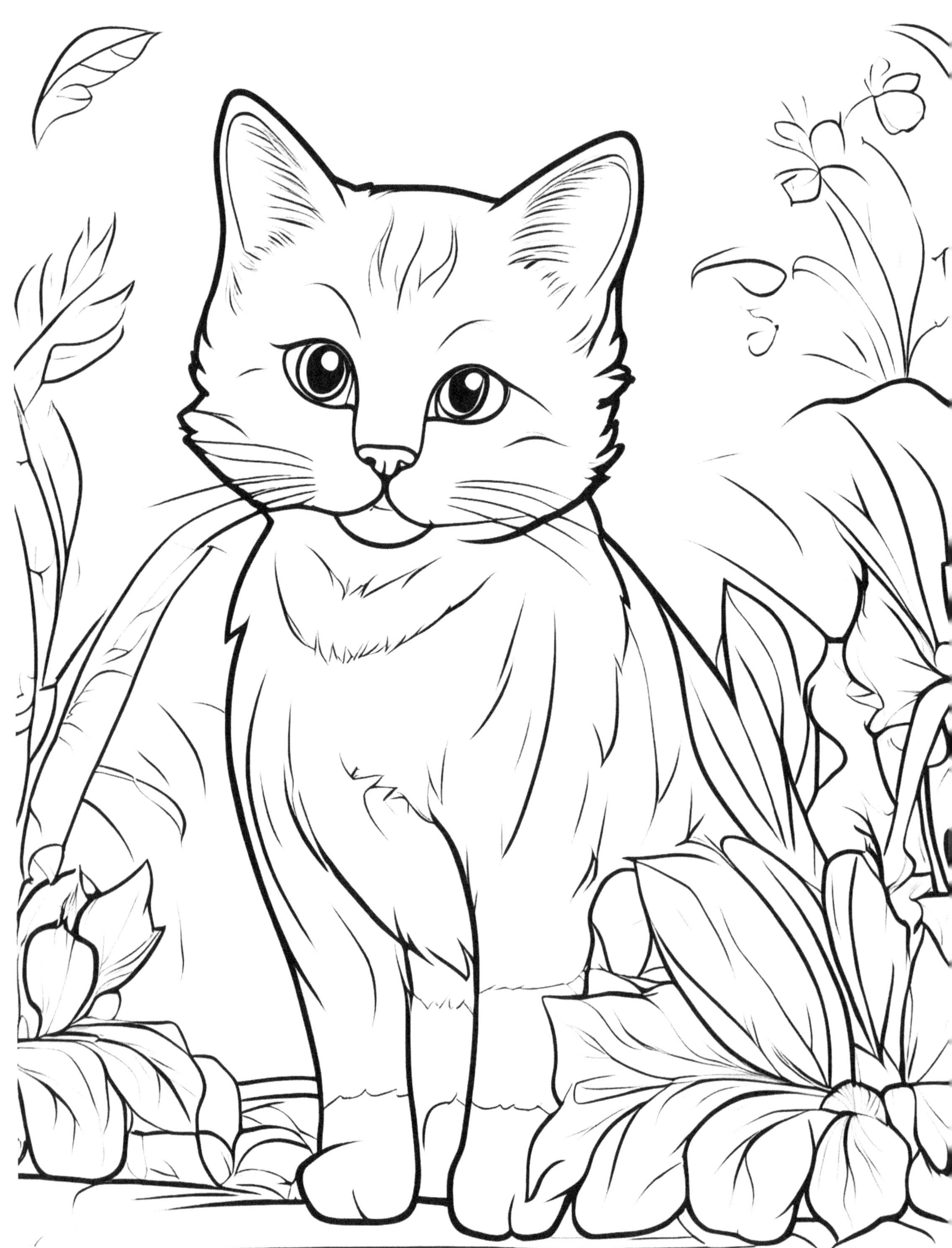

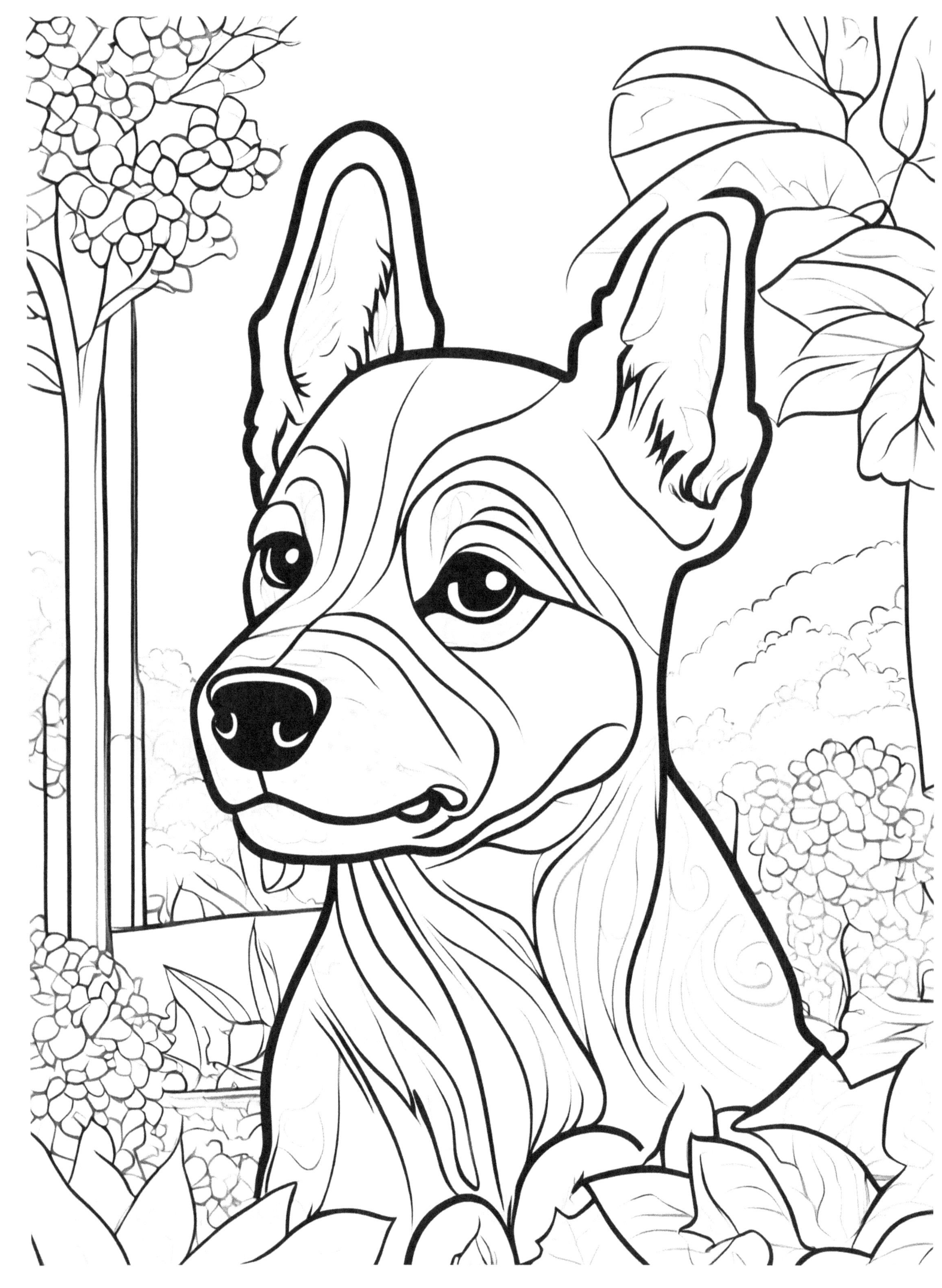

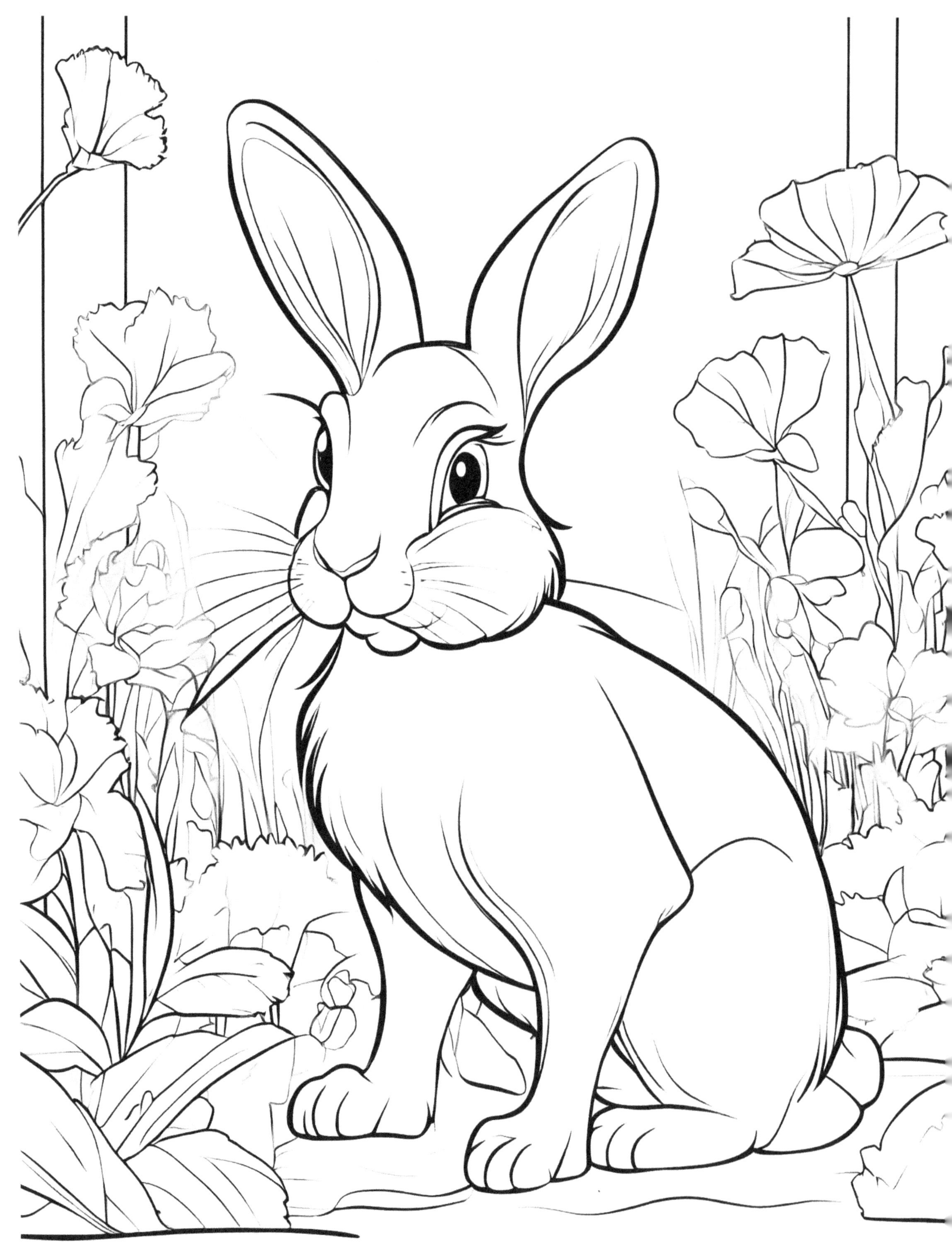

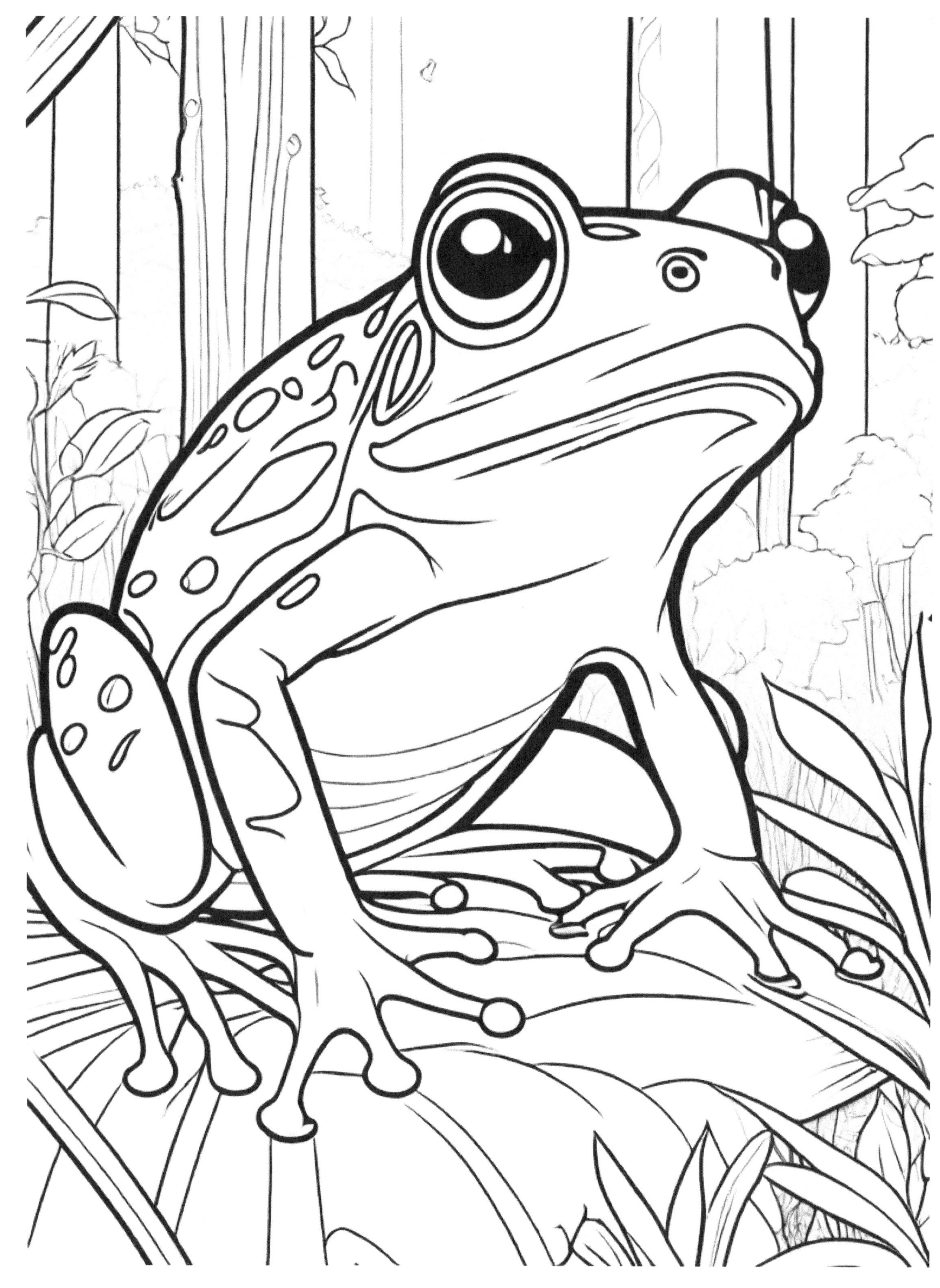

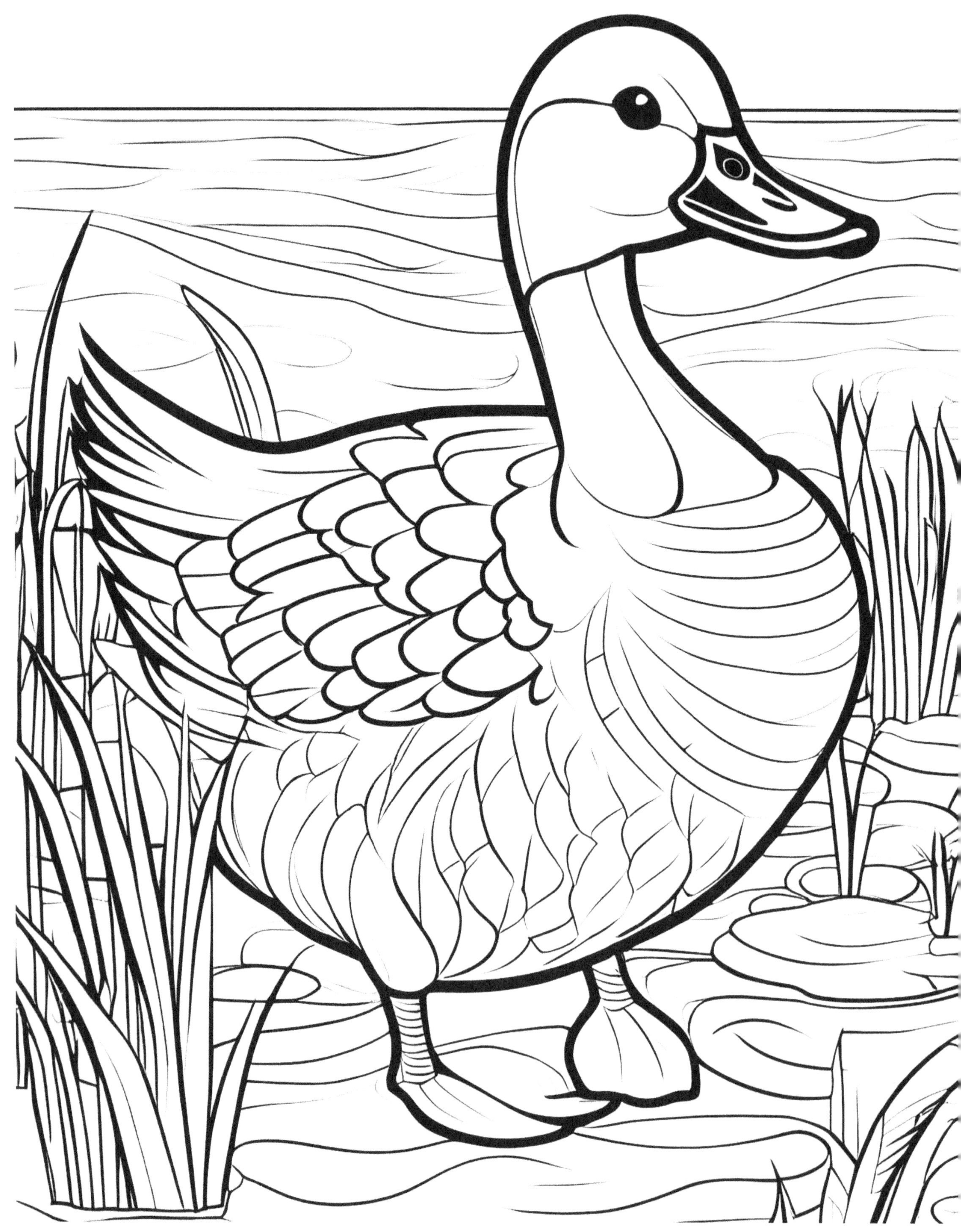

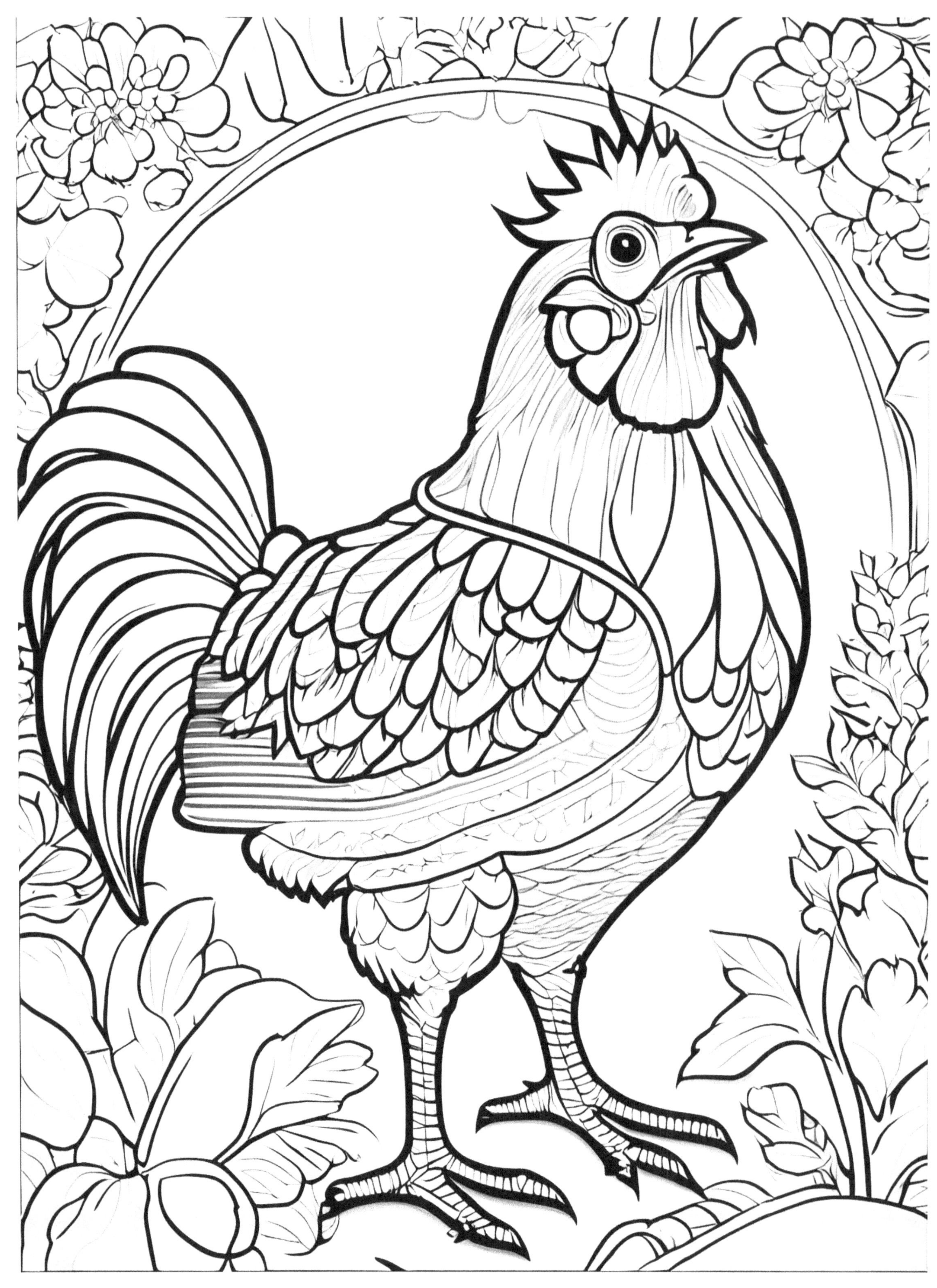

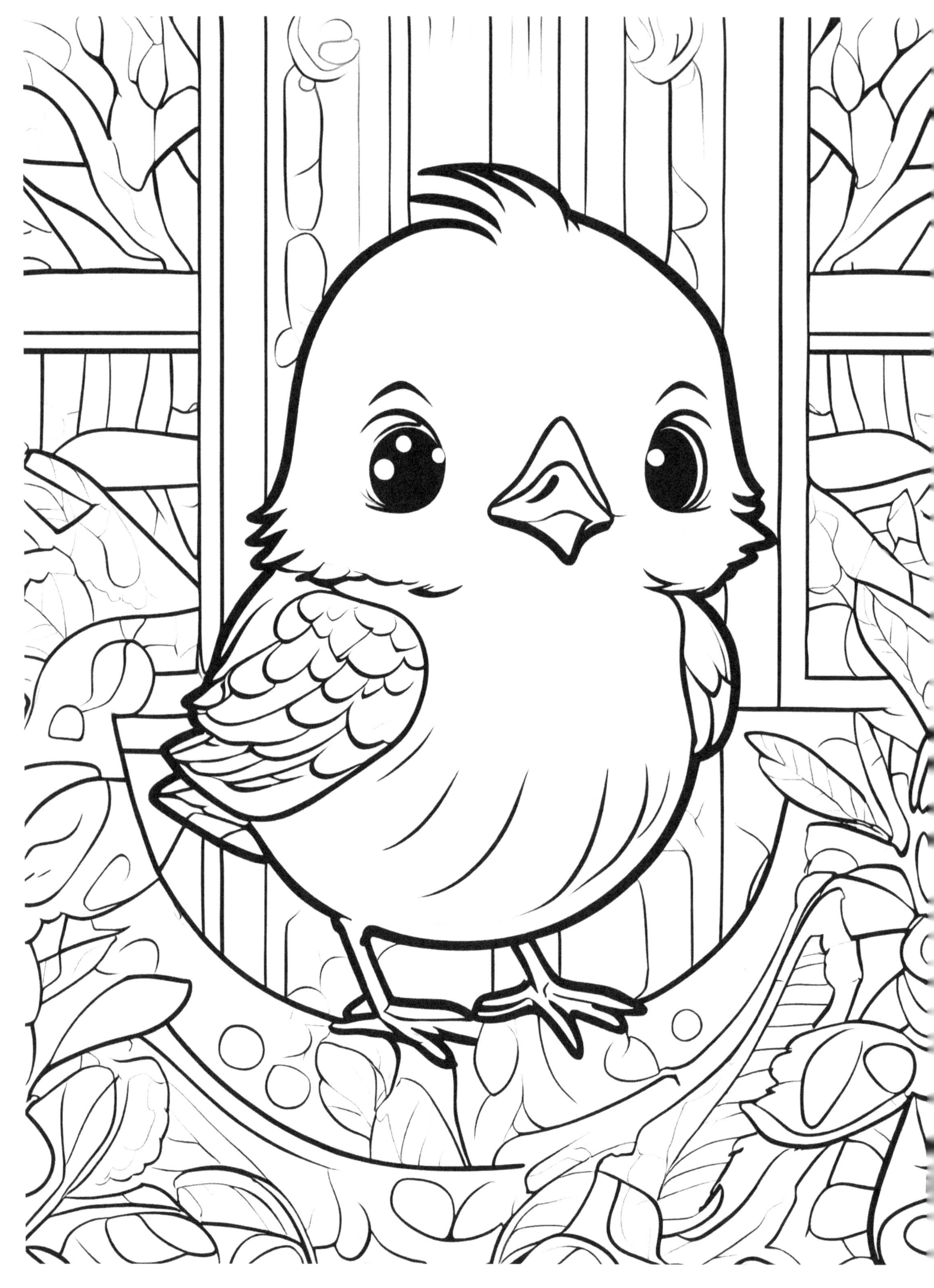

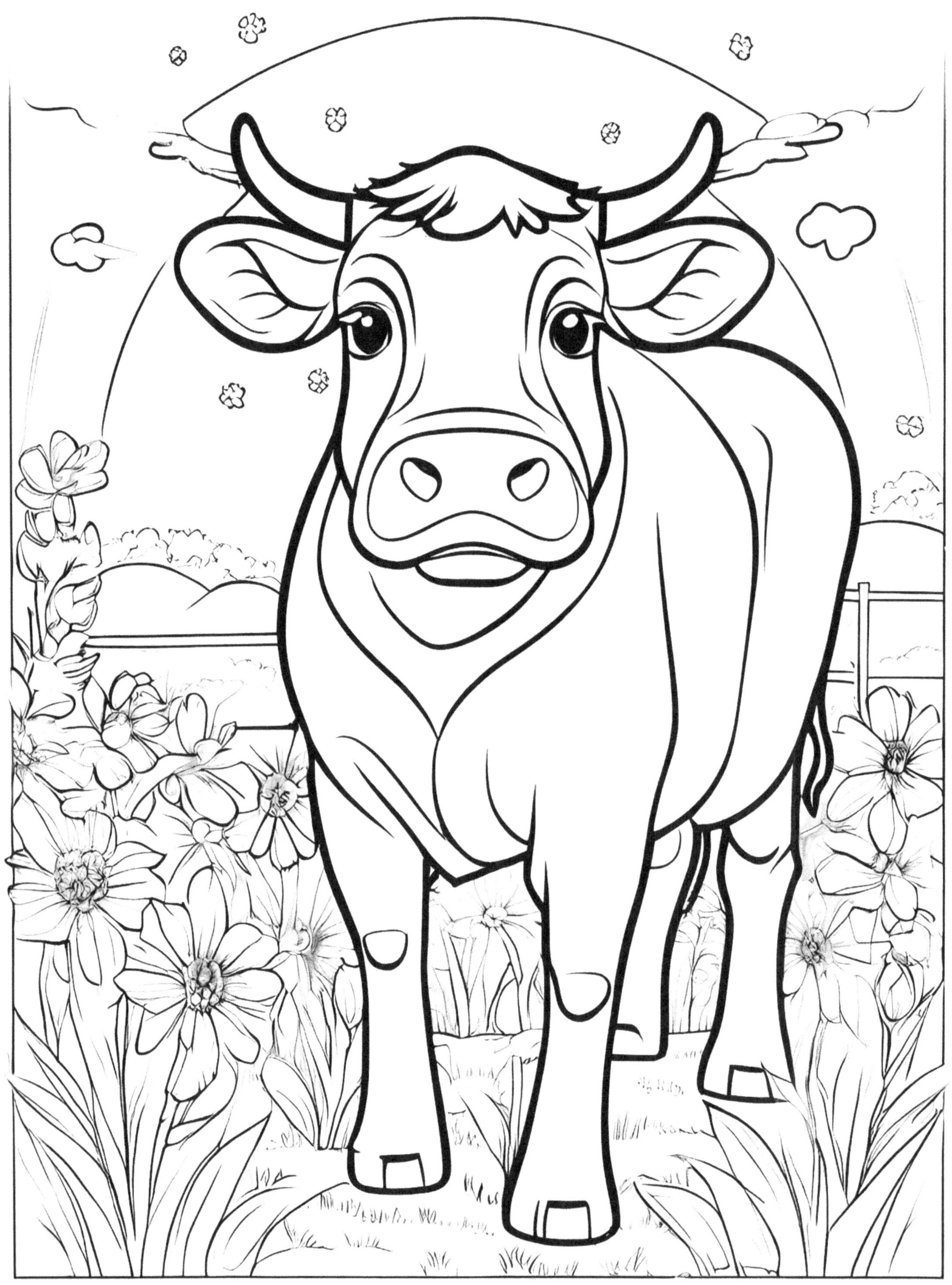

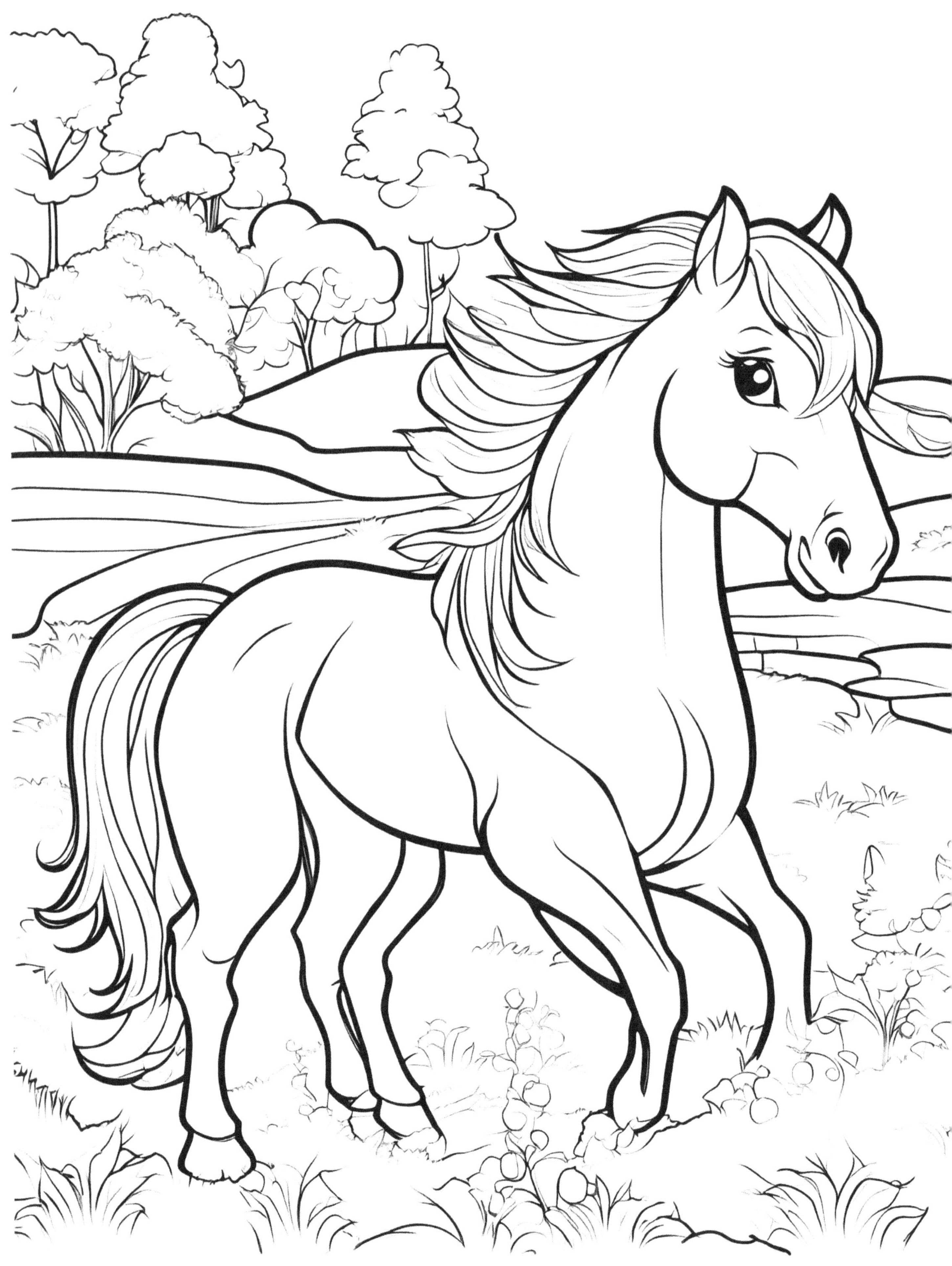

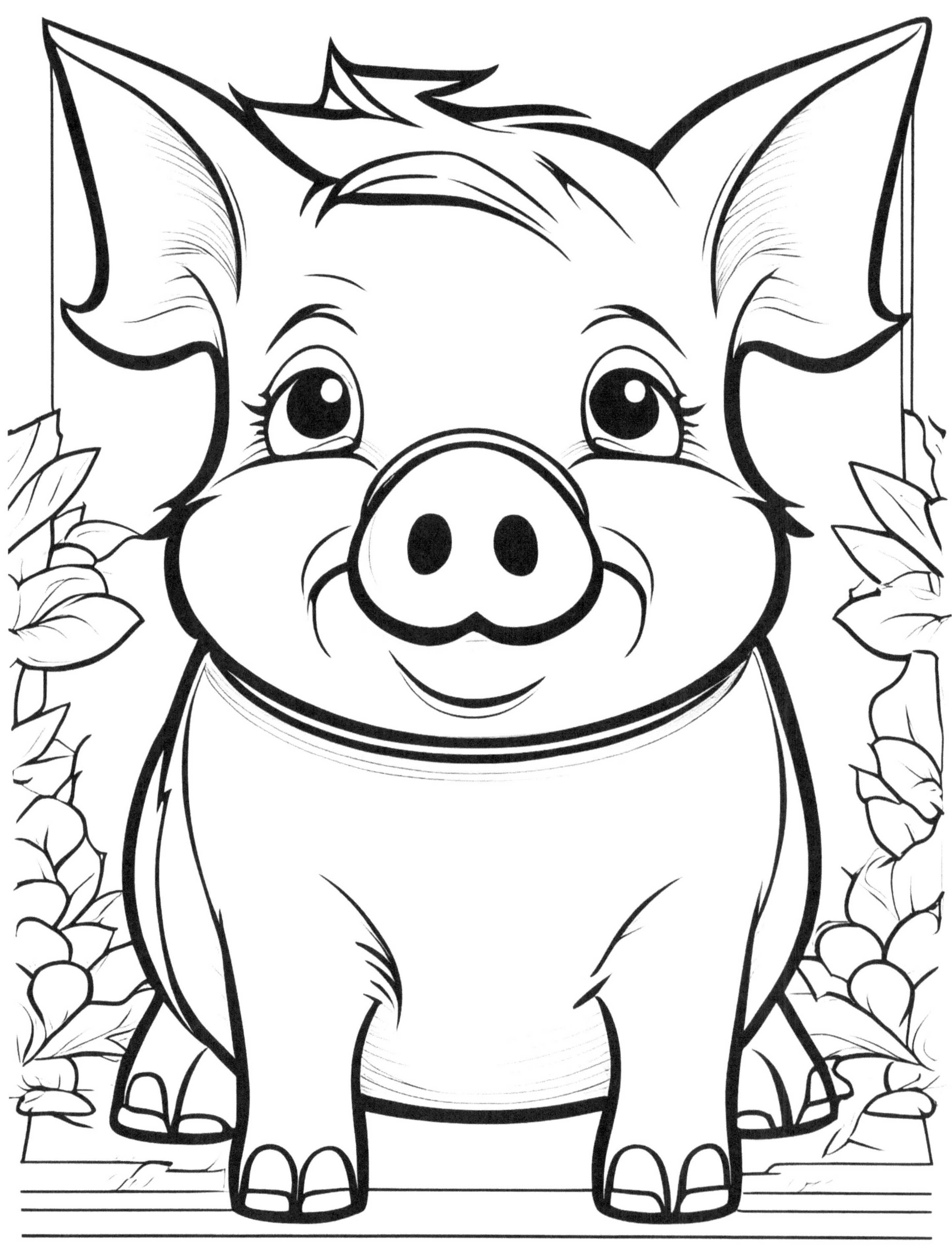

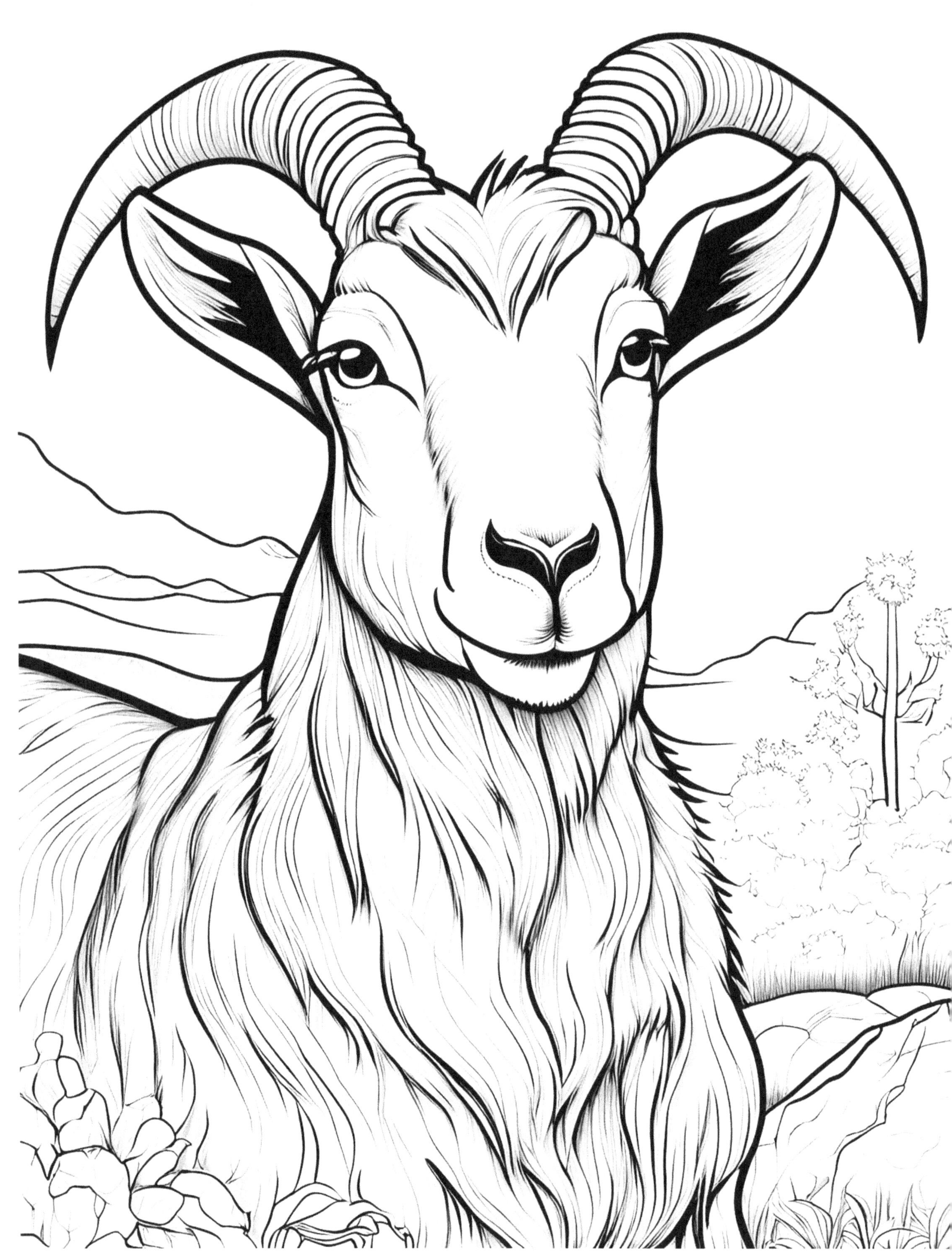

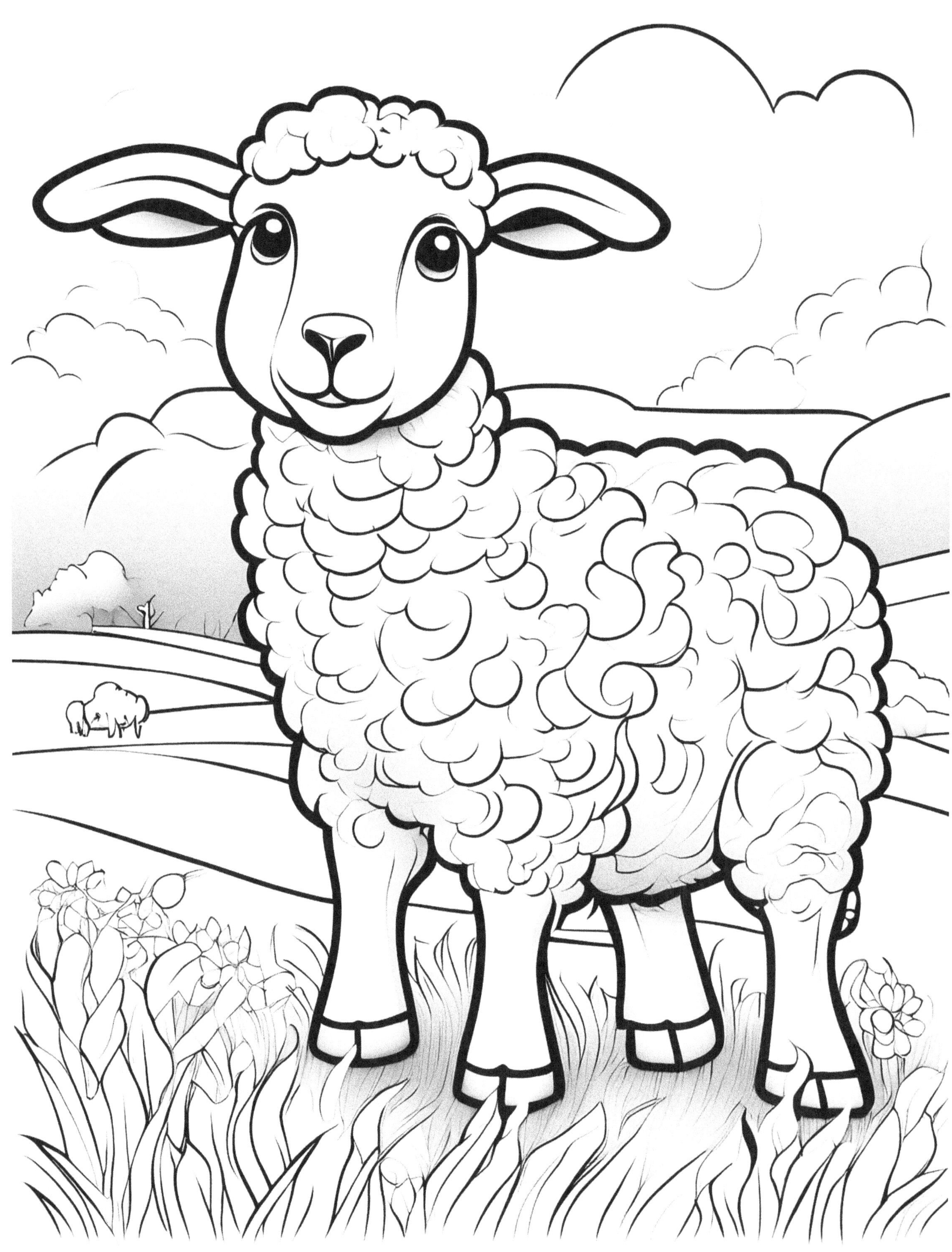

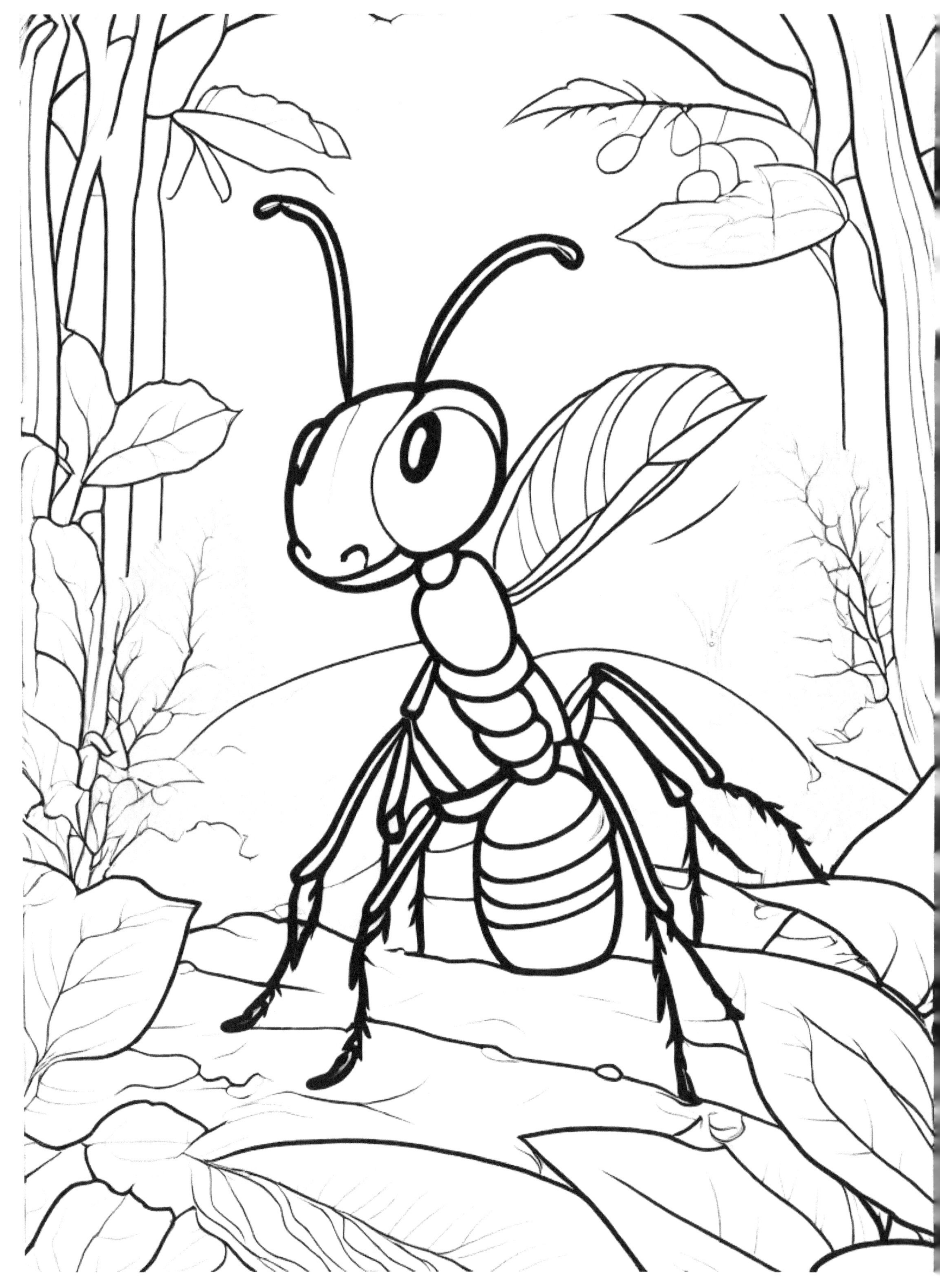

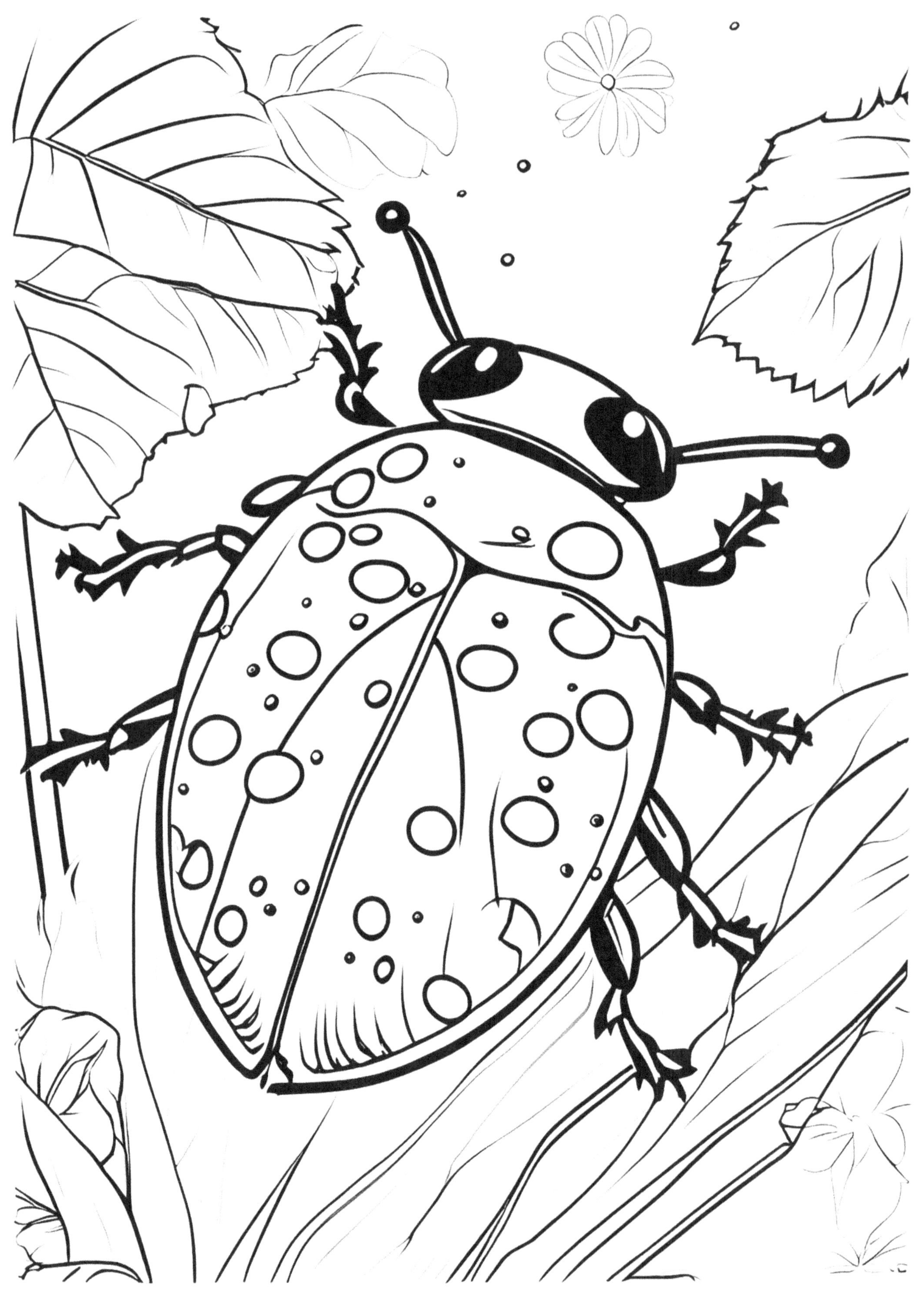

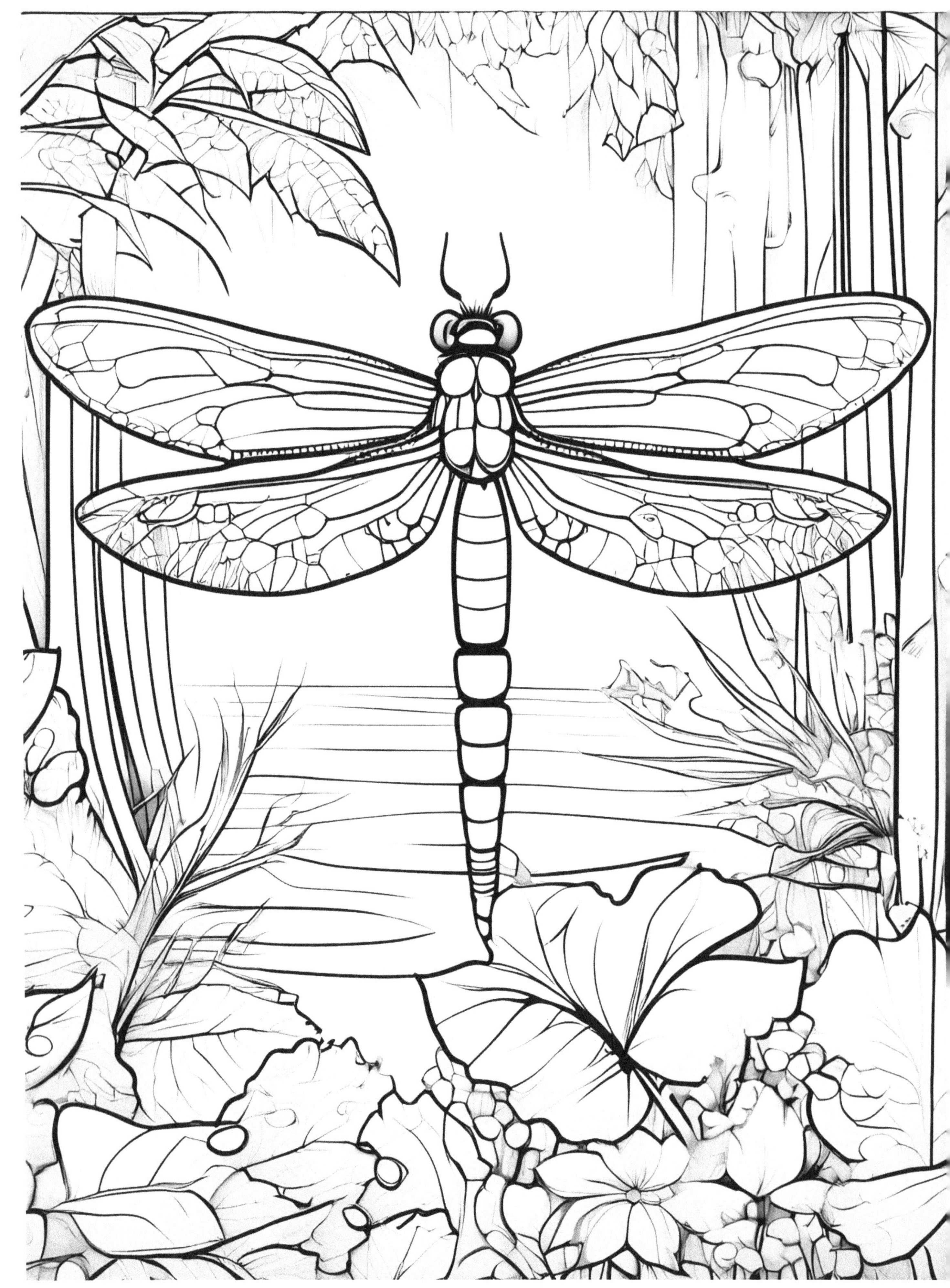

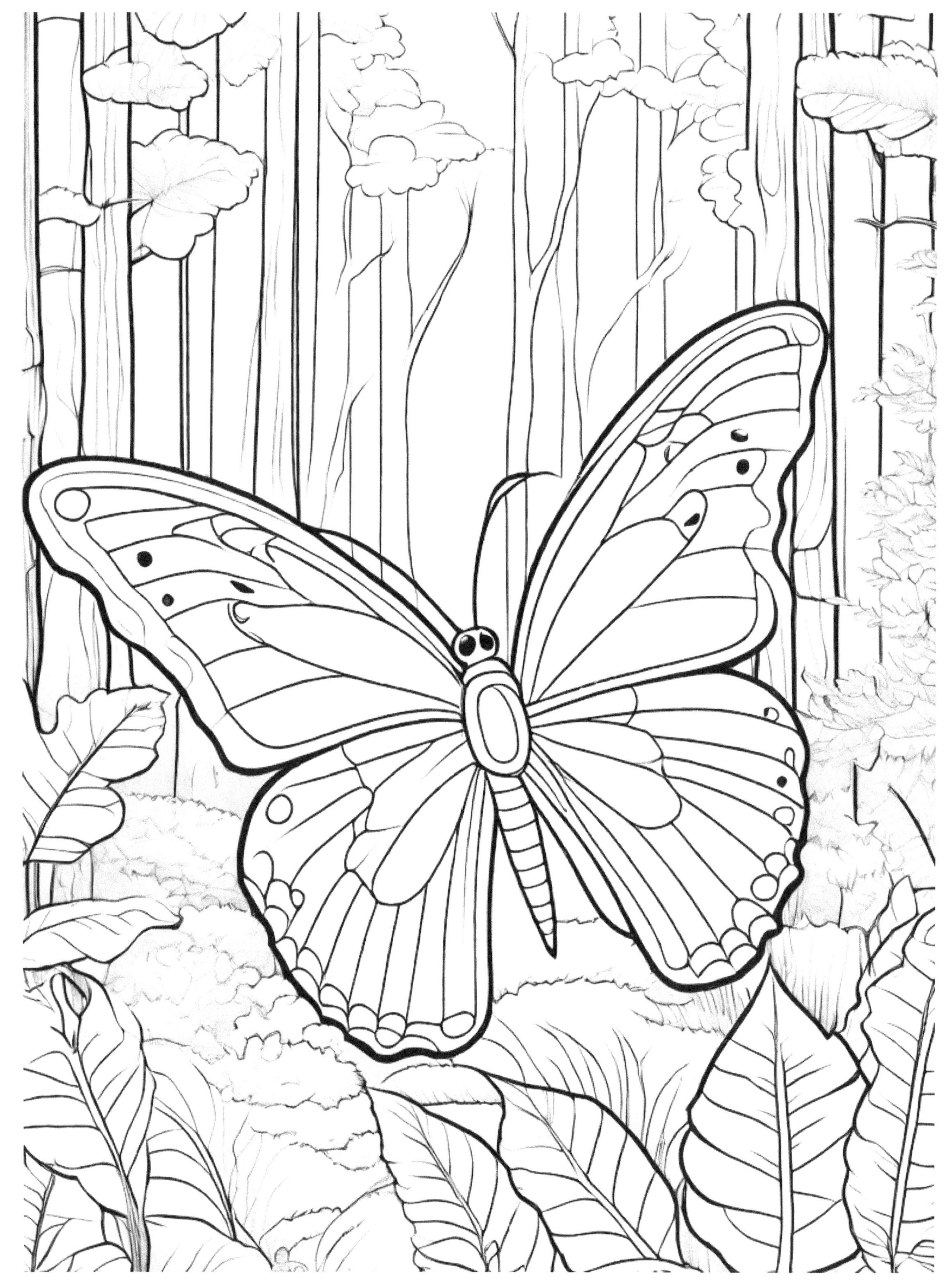

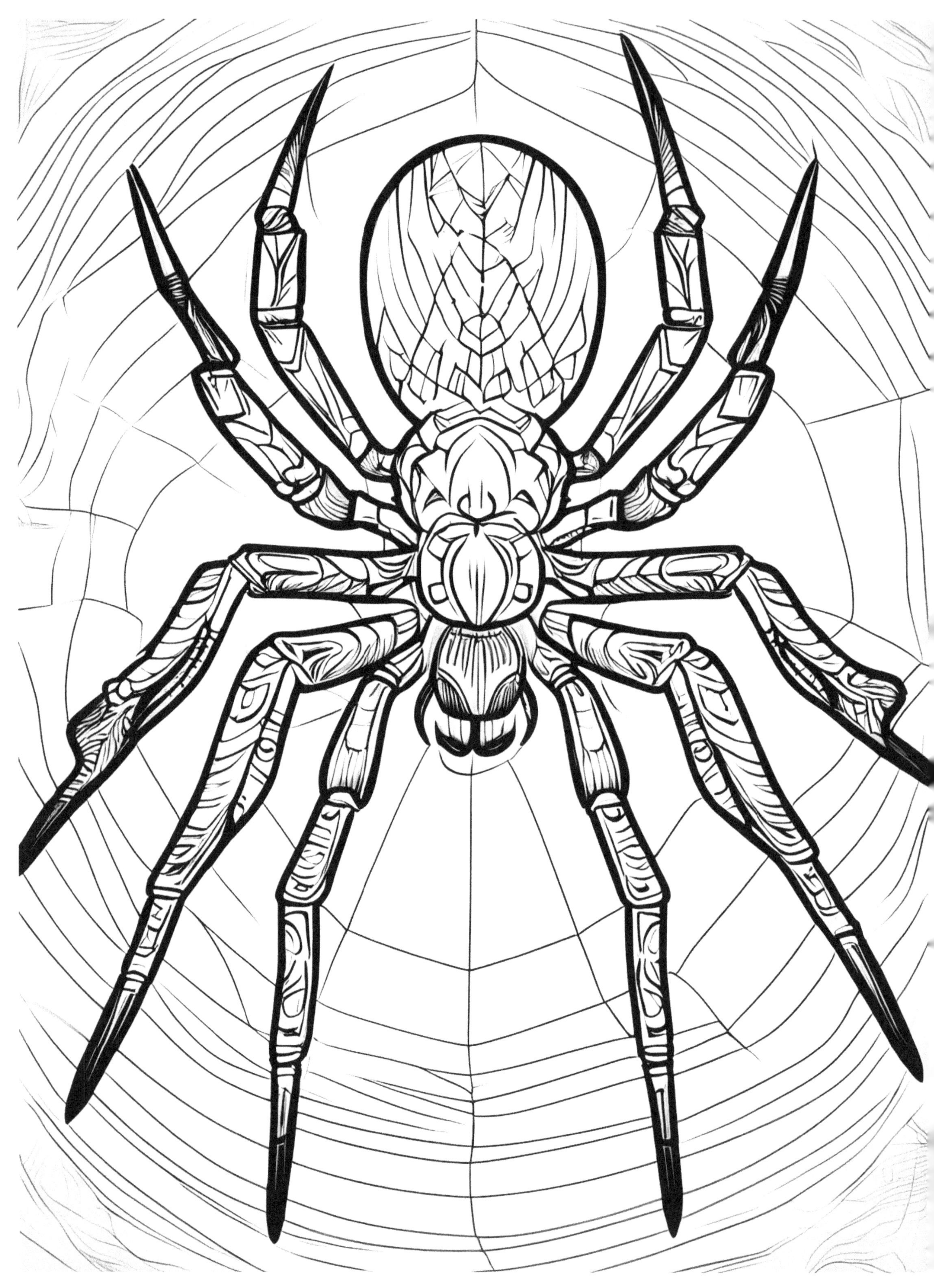

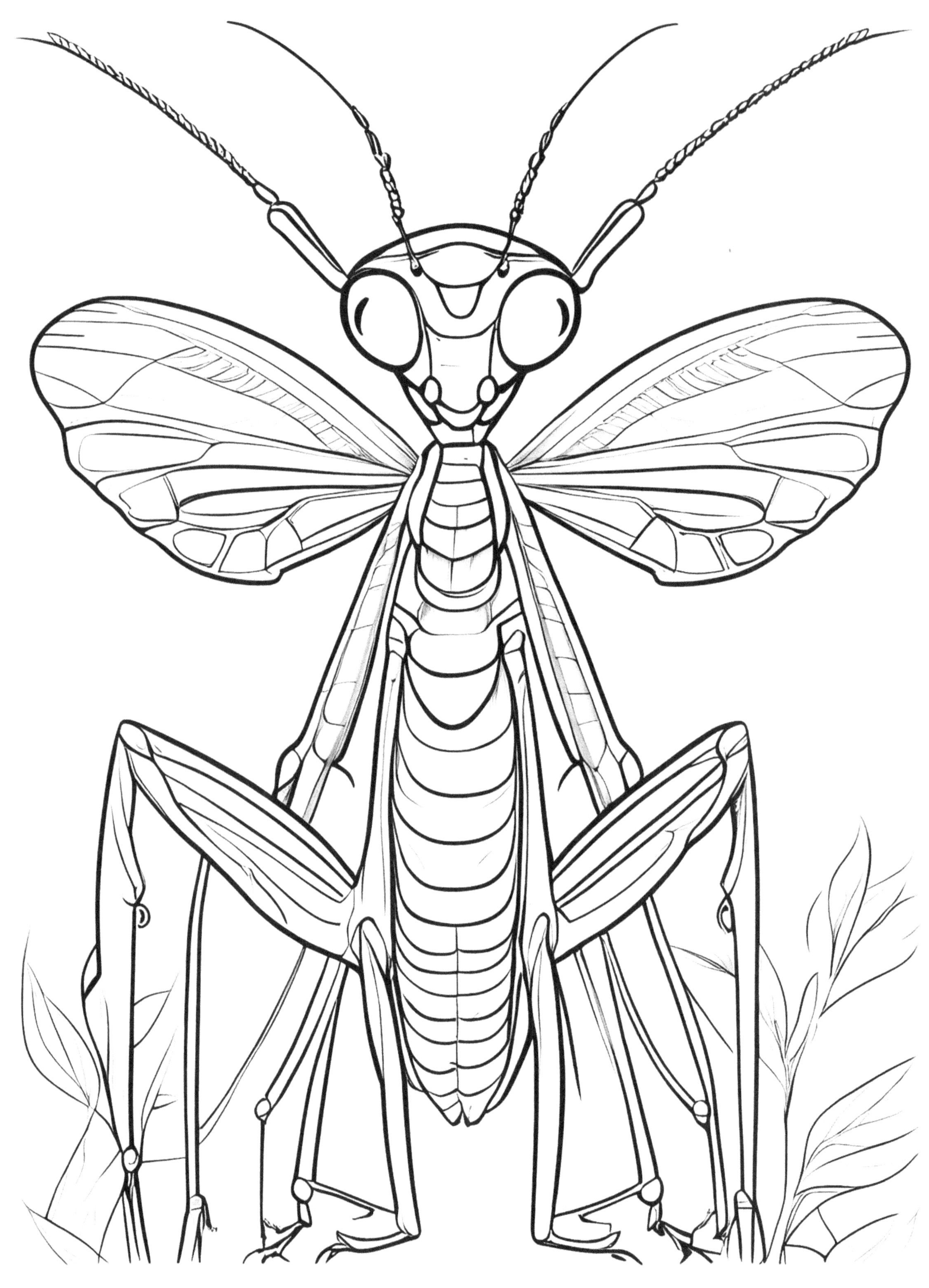

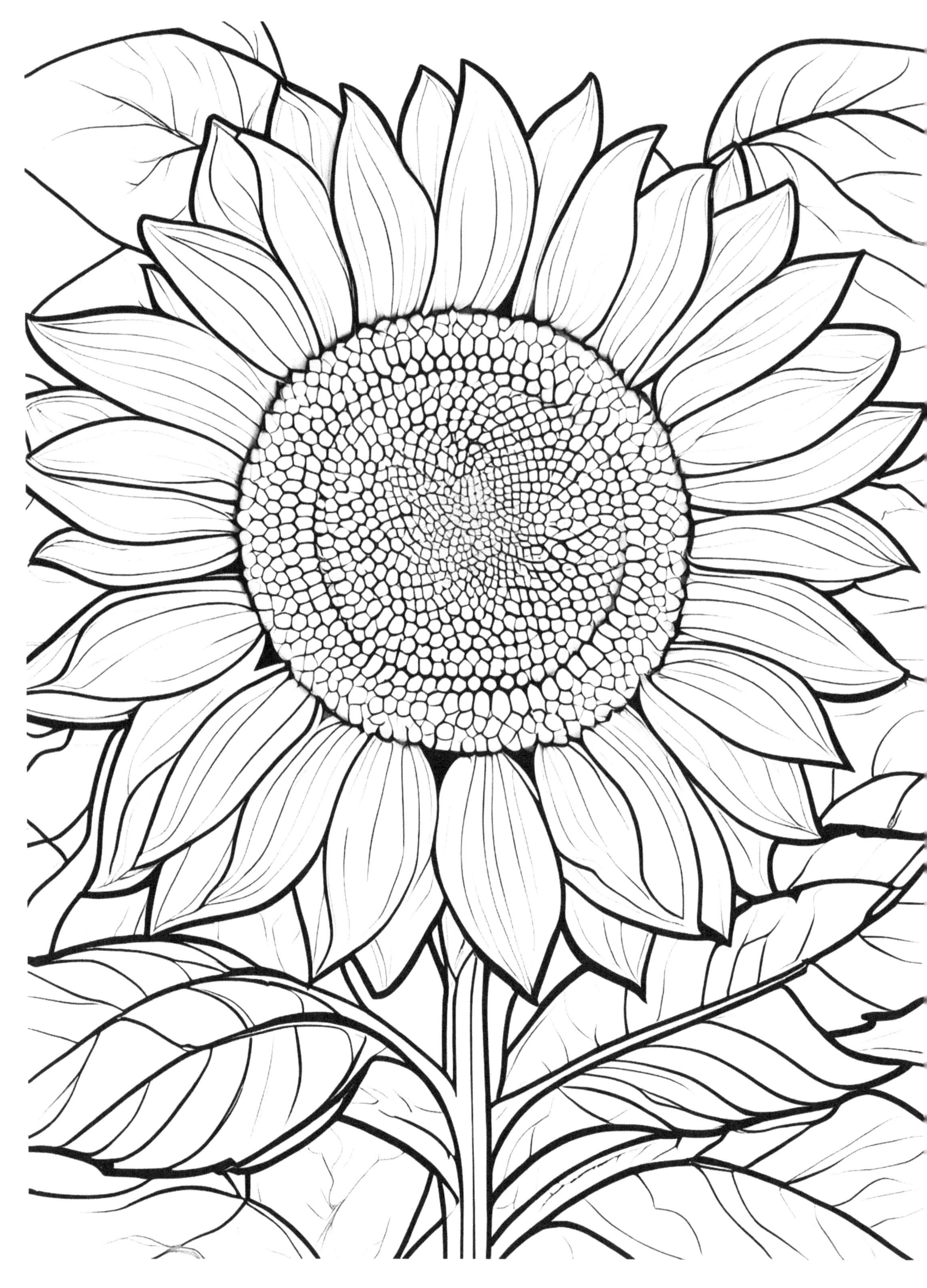

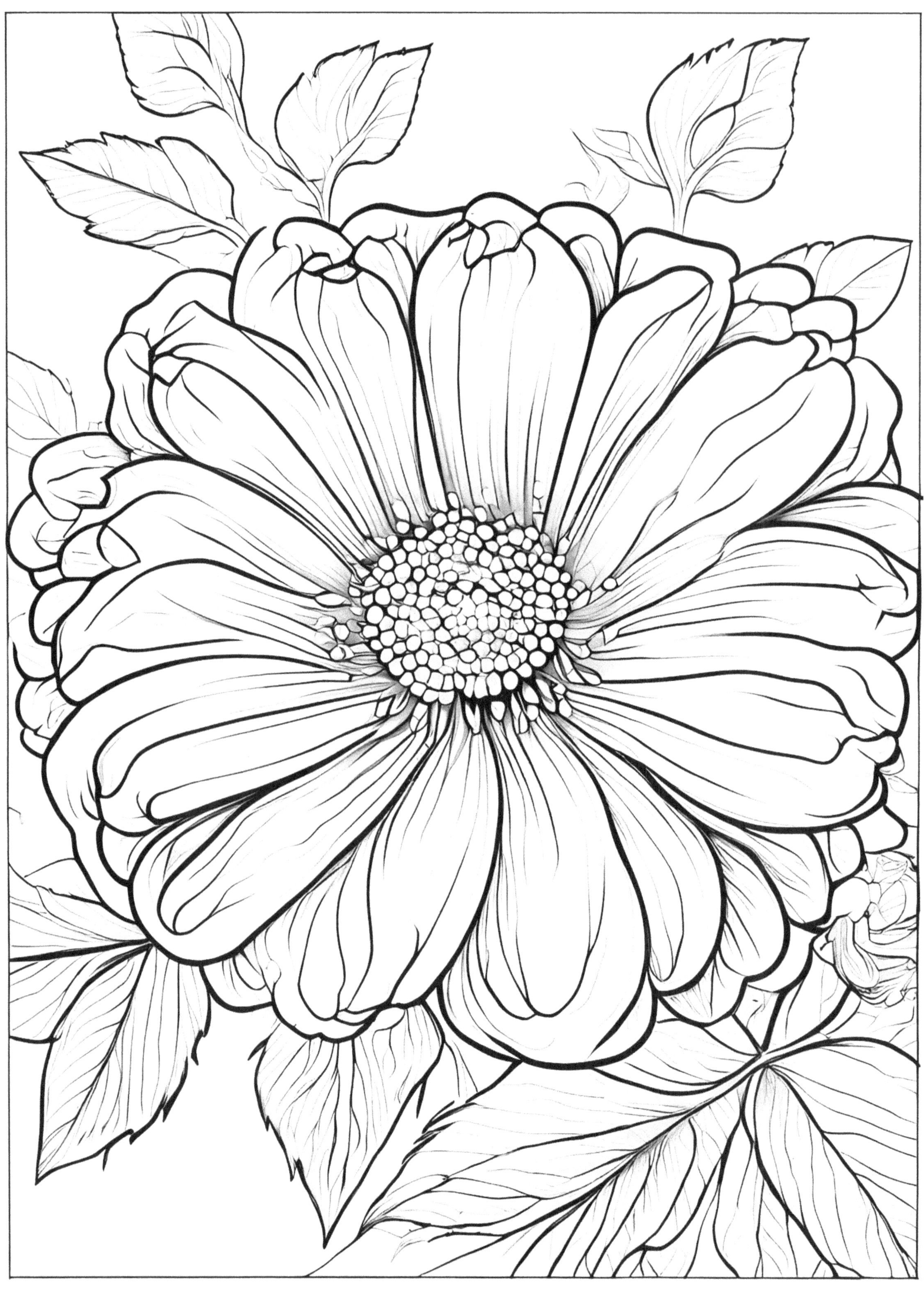

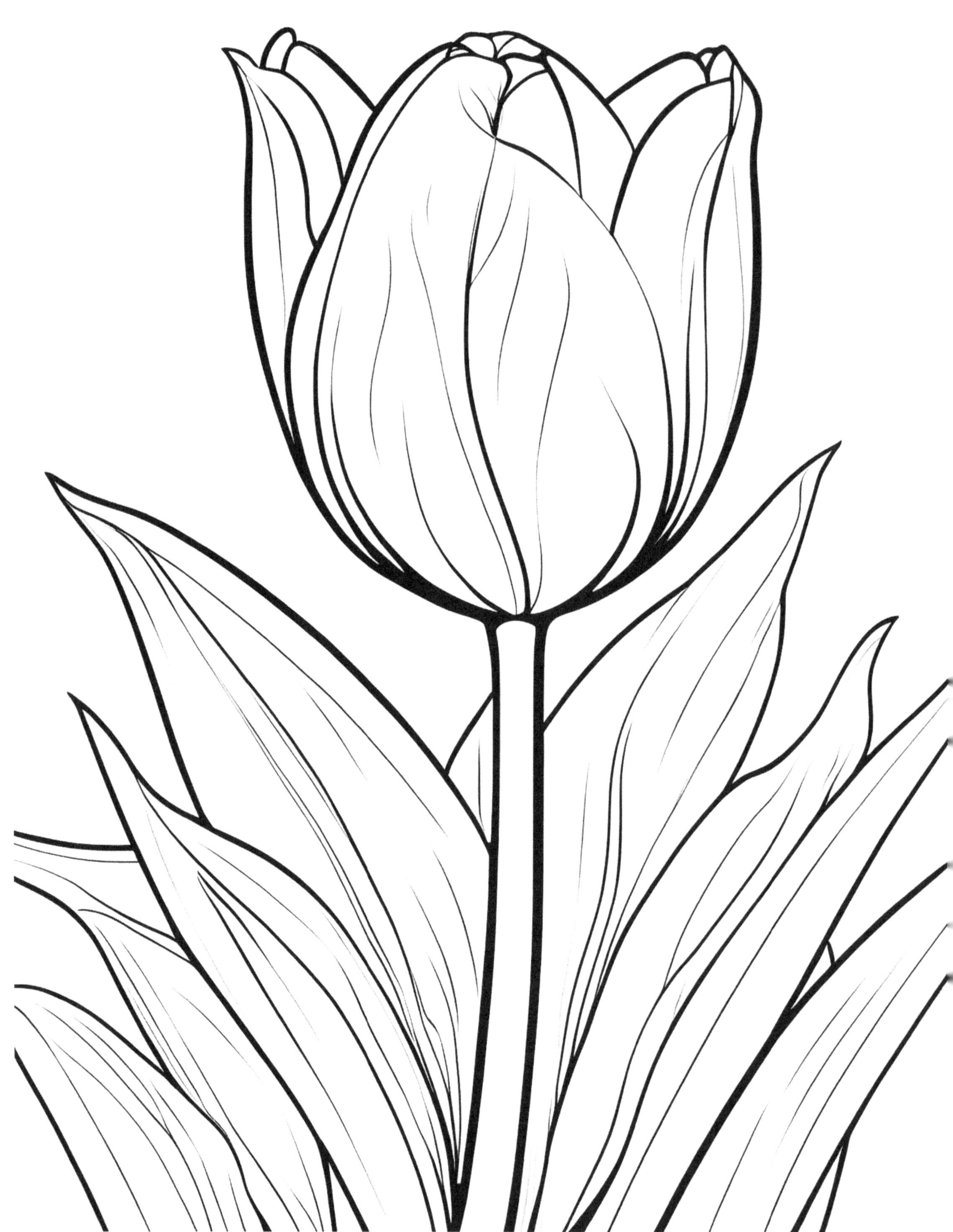

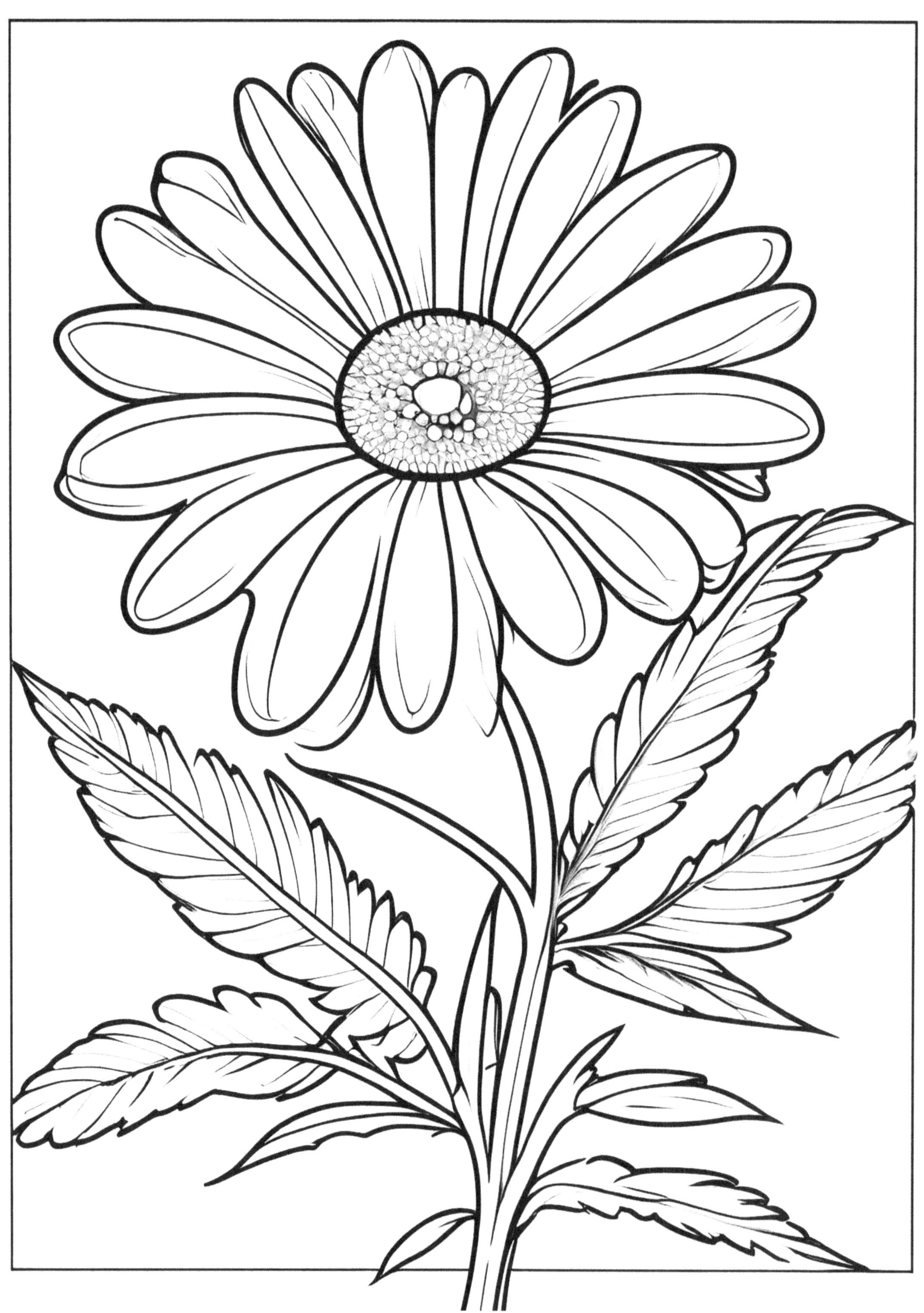

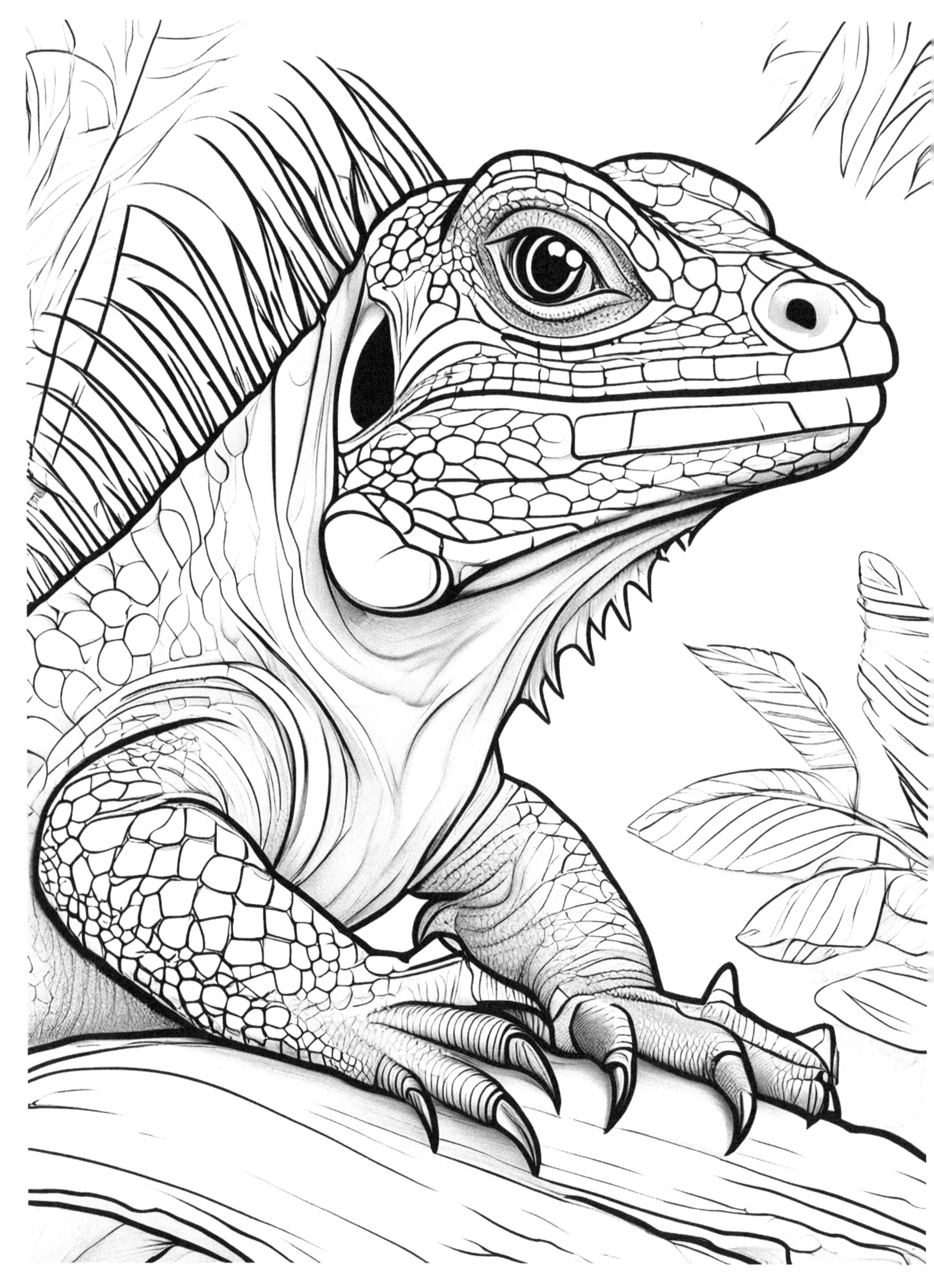

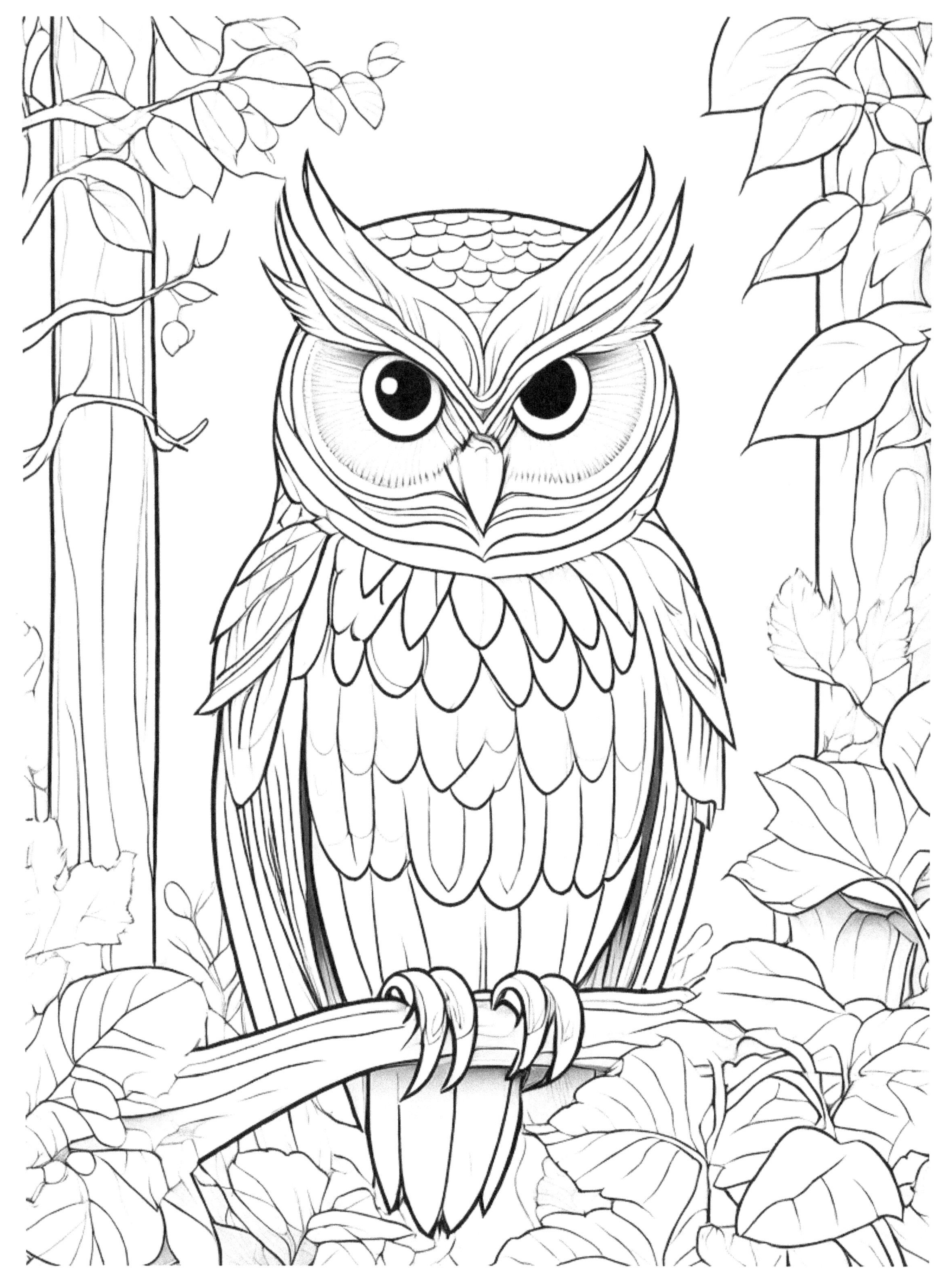

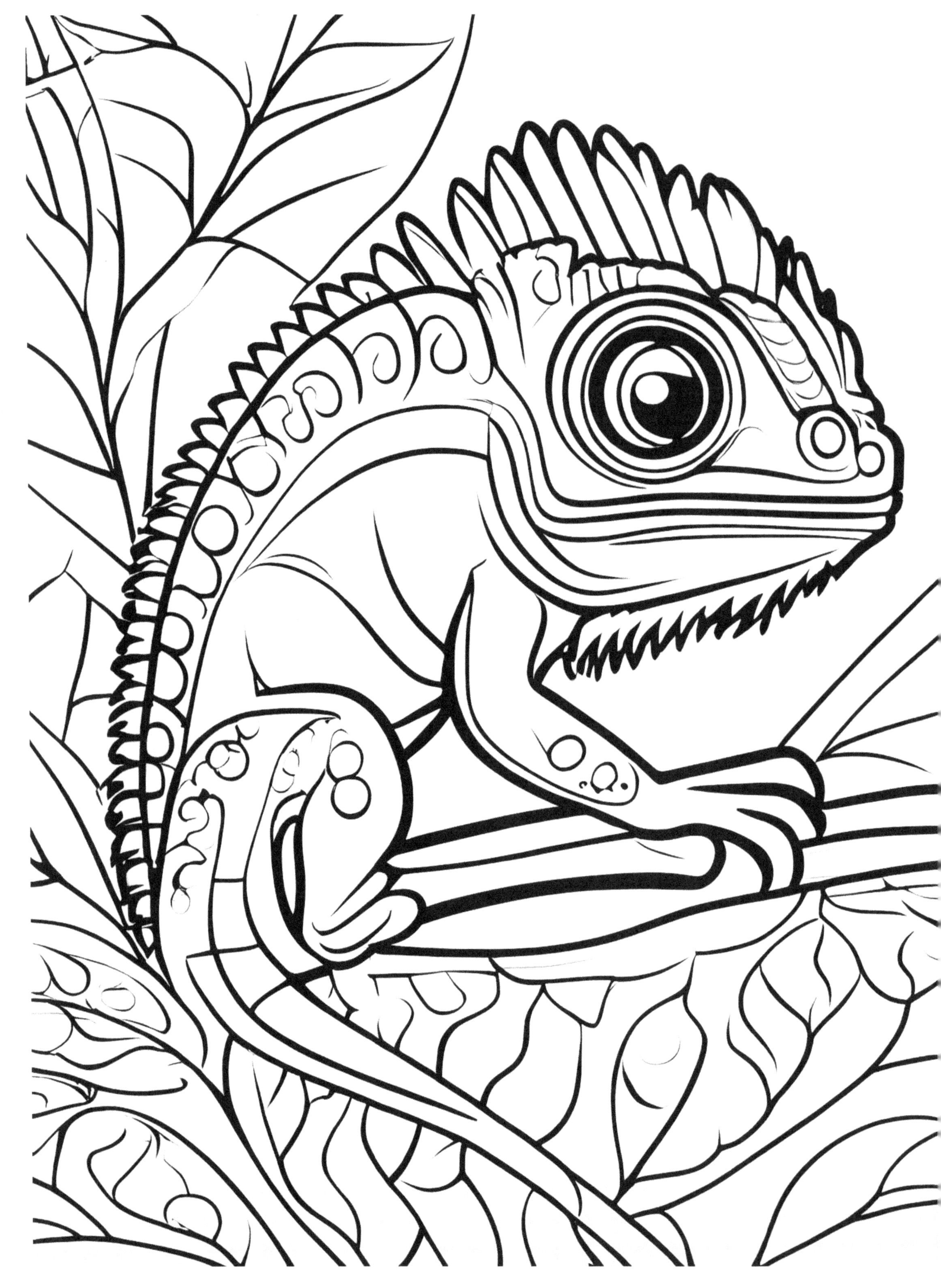

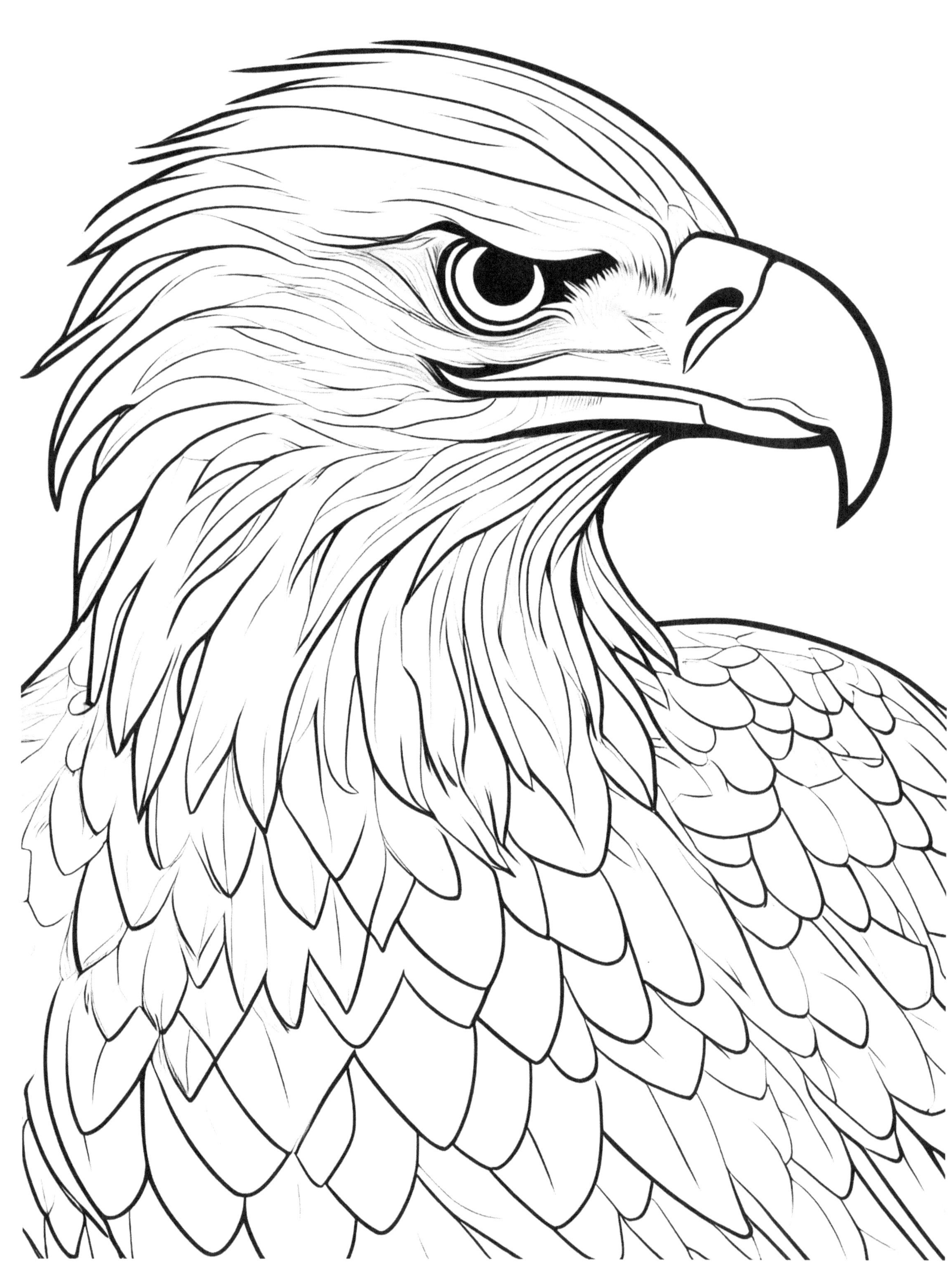

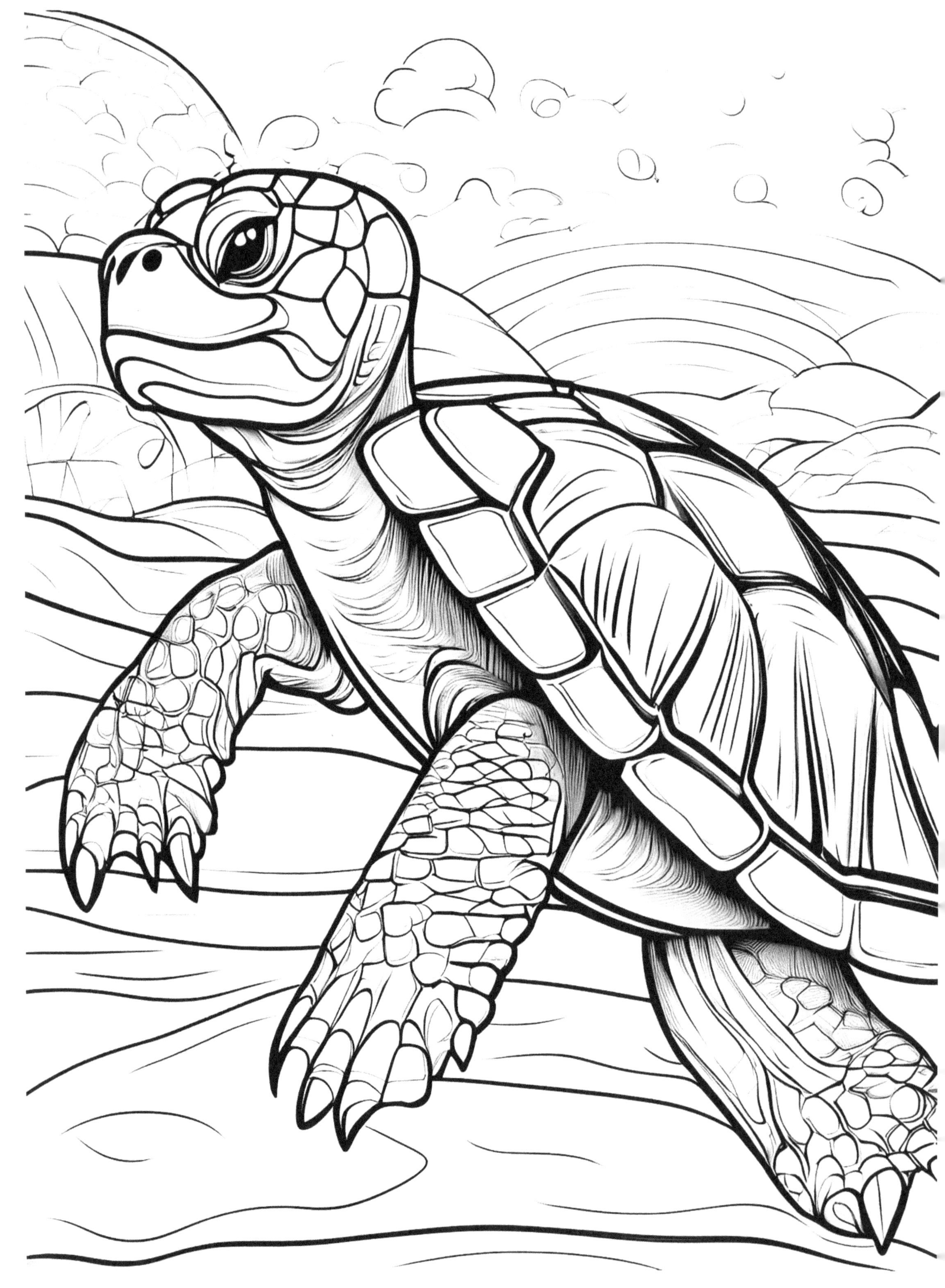

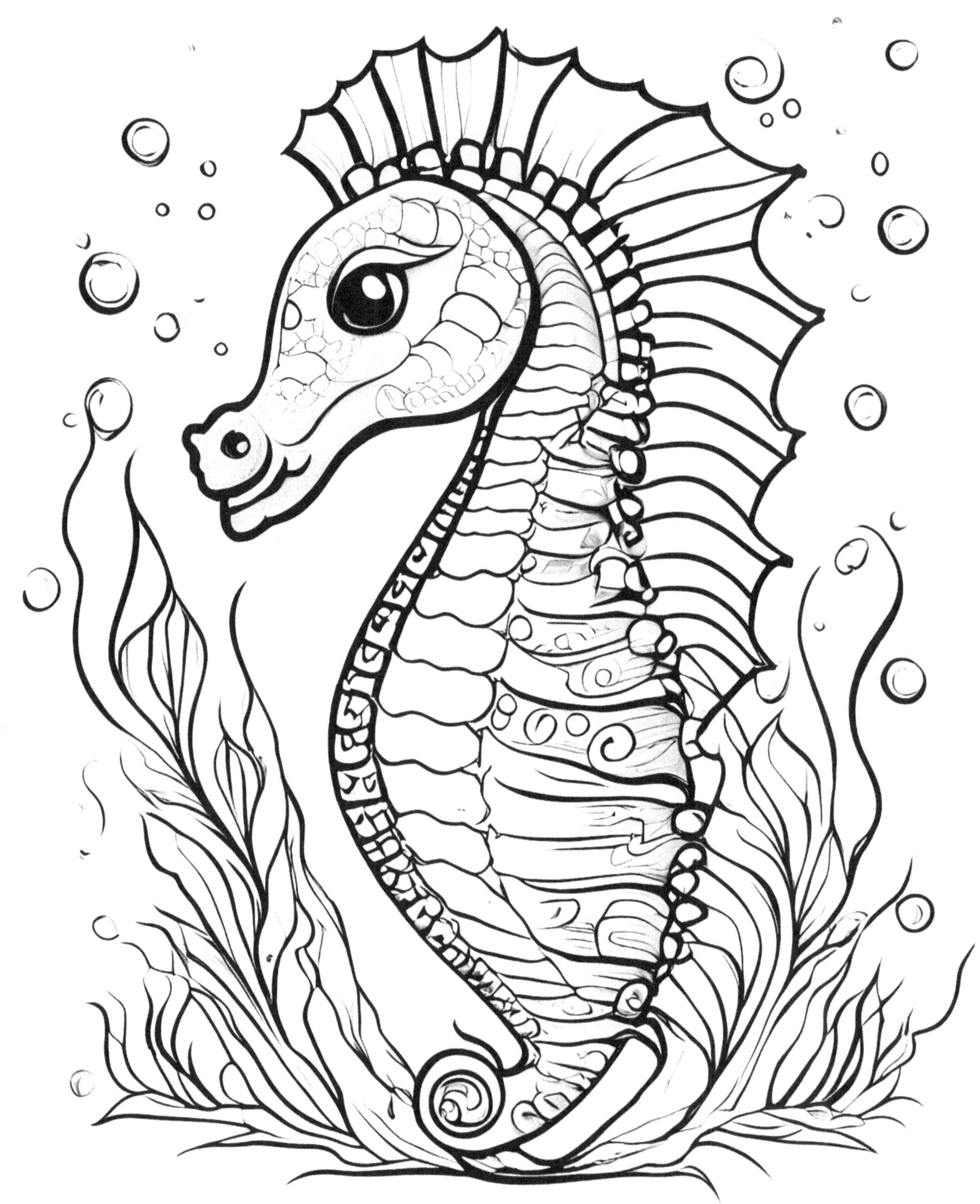

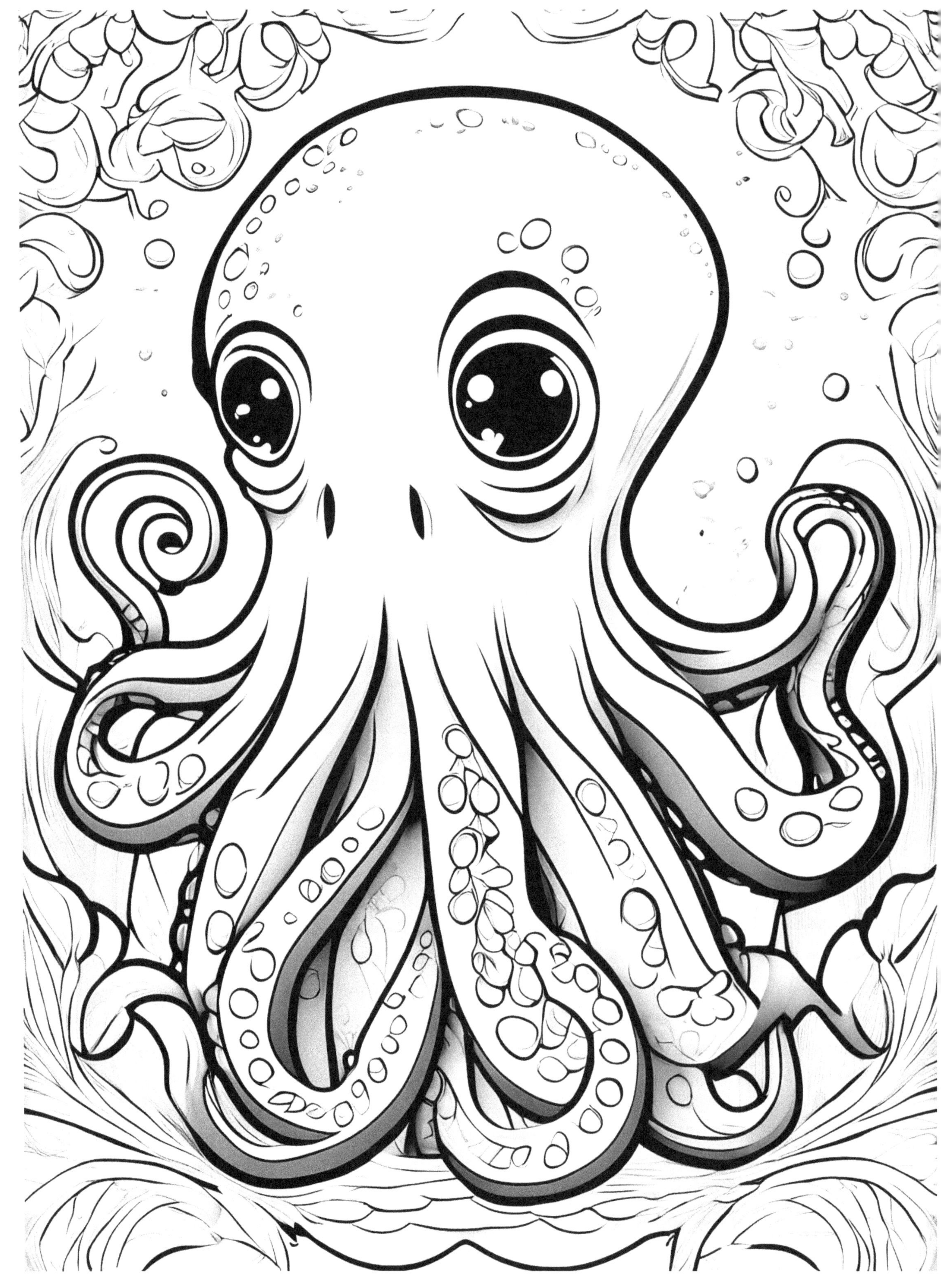

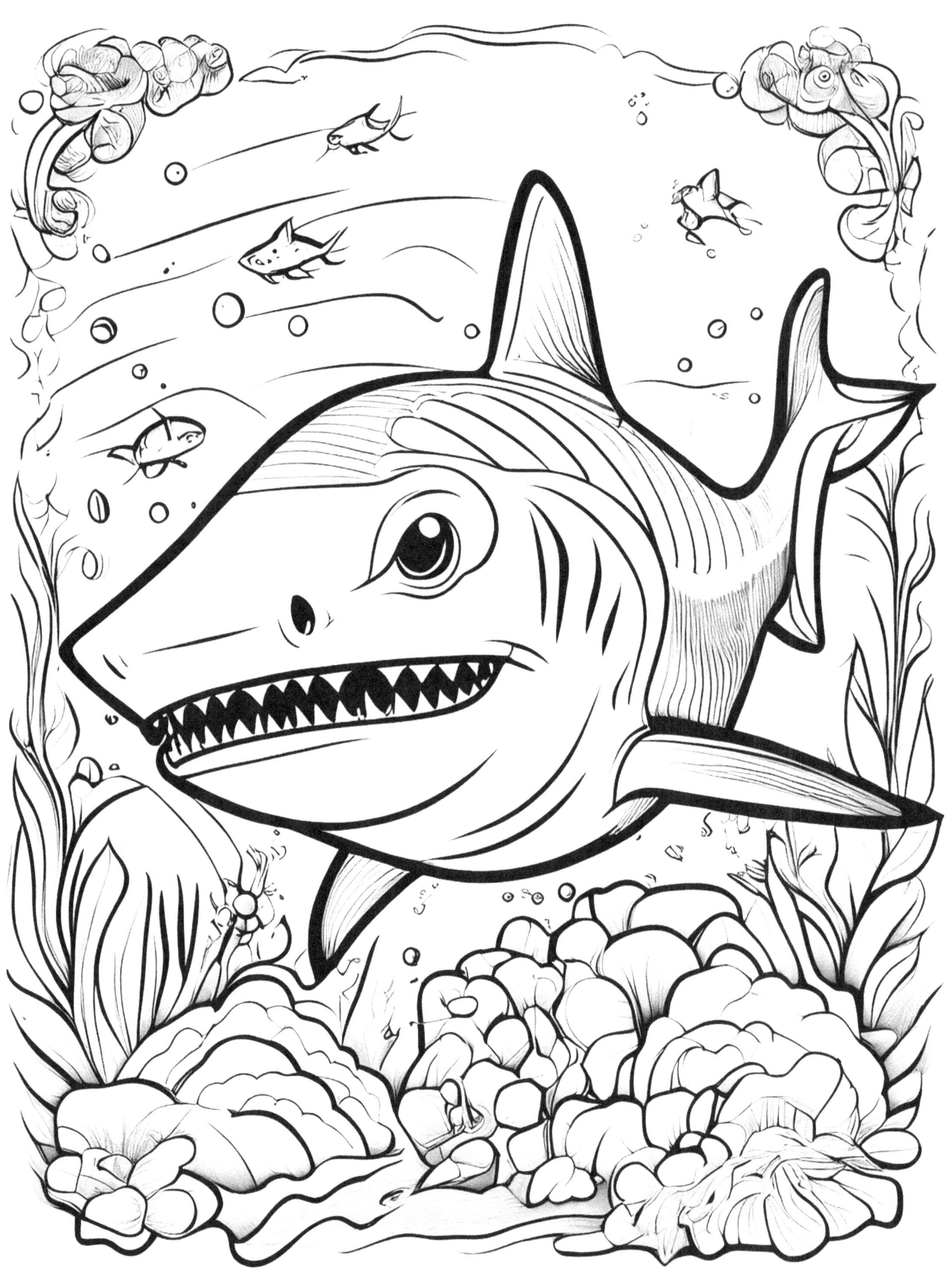